Lillian Too
Jennifer Too

FORTUNE & FENG SHUI

2 0 2 0

KONSEPBOOKS
ASTROLOGY . FENG SHUI . INSPIRATIONS

FORTUNE & FENG SHUI 2020 RAT
by *Lillian Too* and *Jennifer Too*
© 2020 Konsep Lagenda Sdn Bhd

Text © 2020 Lillian Too and Jennifer Too
Photographs and illustrations © Konsep Lagenda Sdn Bhd

The moral right of the authors to be identified as authors of this book
has been asserted.

Published by KONSEP LAGENDA SDN BHD (223 855)
Kuala Lumpur 59100 Malaysia

For more Konsep books, go to *www.lillian-too.com* or *www.wofs.com*
To report errors, please send a note to errors@konsepbooks.com
For general feedback, email feedback@konsepbooks.com

Notice of Rights
All rights reserved. No part of this publication may be reproduced,
stored in a retrieval system or transmitted in any form, or by any
means, electronic, mechanical, photocopying, recording, or otherwise,
without the prior written permission of the publisher.
For information on getting permission for reprints and excerpts,
contact: permissions@konsepbooks.com

Notice of Liability
The information in this book is distributed on an "As Is" basis, without
warranty. While every precaution has been taken in the preparation
of the book, neither the author nor Konsep Lagenda shall have any
liability to any person or entity with respect to any loss or damage
caused or alleged to be caused directly or indirectly by the instructions
contained in this book.

ISBN 978-967-329-269-1
Published in Malaysia, September 2019

RAT 2020

BIRTH YEAR	WESTERN CALENDAR DATES	AGE	KUA NUMBER MALES	KUA NUMBER FEMALES
Wood Rat	5 Feb 1924 - 23 Jan 1925	96	4 East Group	2 West Group
Fire Rat	24 Jan 1936 - 10 Feb 1937	84	1 East Group	5/8 West Group
Earth Rat	10 Feb 1948 - 28 Jan 1949	72	7 West Group	8 West Group
Metal Rat	28 Jan 1960 - 14 Feb 1961	60	4 East Group	2 West Group
Water Rat	15 Feb 1972 - 2 Feb 1973	48	1 East Group	5/8 West Group
Wood Rat	2 Feb 1984 - 19 Feb 1985	36	7 West Group	8 West Group
Fire Rat	19 Feb 1996 - 6 Feb 1997	24	4 East Group	2 West Group
Earth Rat	7 Feb 2008 - 25 Jan 2009	12	1 East Group	5/8 West Group

CONTENTS

CONTENTS

CHAPTER ONE
OUTLOOK FOR YEAR 2020   8
Metal Rat Year 2020   9
Feng Shui Chart of 2020   16
The Presence of Lap Chun   20
Outlook for the 12 Animals   22
24 Mountains Chart of 2020   23

CHAPTER TWO
FOUR PILLARS CHART 2020   28
Paht Chee Chart of 2020   29
Hidden Stars of 2020   36
Star of Scholastic Brilliance   38
Commanding Star   41
Star of Powerful Mentors   44
Importance of a Strong Life Force   46
Strengthening Success Luck in 2020   48

CHAPTER THREE
LUCK OF THE RAT IN 2020   51
Element Luck of the Rat 2020   52
12 Year Old Earth Rat   58
24 Year Old Fire Rat   59
36 Year Old Wood Rat   60
48 Year Old Water Rat   61
60 Year Old Metal Rat   62
72 Year Old Earth Rat   63
84 Year Old Fire Rat   65

CONTENTS

CHAPTER FOUR

FLYING STAR CHART OF 2020   68

Dealing with #7 in the Center   76

Beware Quarrelsome Star #3 in the North   83

East plays host to Five Yellow   87

Illness Star made worse by Fire in the South   89

Prosperity originates in Northwest this year   93

West represents Long-Term Gains   99

Northeast enjoys Winning Luck   104

Southeast blessed by the Heavens   107

Peach Blossom Luck in the Southwest   112

Southwest also brings scholastic success   116

Tai Sui in the North   120

Three Killings in the South   123

CHAPTER FIVE

RAT COMPATIBILITIES IN 2020   126

Getting along despite your argumentative nature 127

Short vs Long Run Compatibility   128

Affinity Triangle of Competitors   130

Astrological Soulmates - Rat and Ox   133

Secret Friends - Rat and Ox   135

Seasonal Combination of Winter   137

Peach Blossom Link with the Rooster   139

Your Zodiac Enemy - the Horse   140

RAT'S RELATIONSHIPS WITH OTHER SIGNS IN 2020

	143
RAT/RAT - Quarrelsome but auspicious time	144
RAT/OX - Rat benefits from Ox's restful nature	146
RAT/TIGER - Tiger lends strength to Rat in 2020	148
RAT/RABBIT - A noisy pairing in 2020! Not ideal.	150
RAT/DRAGON - Allies supporting one another	152
RAT/SNAKE - Long-lasting bond	154
RAT/HORSE - Astrological foes in a noisy year!	156
RAT/SHEEP - Rat wrapped round Sheep's little finger	158
RAT/MONKEY - Best of pals on a roll!	160
RAT/ROOSTER - Much bliss & happiness to be had	162
RAT/DOG - Ho Tu combination brings good fortune	164
RAT/BOAR - A happy year for these two	166

CHAPTER SIX
RAT'S MONTH BY MONTH LUCK FOR 2020

	168
Overview for the RAT	169
Feb 2020 - Romantic diversions subdue anger	171
Mar 2020 - Quarrelsome indeed!	174
Apr 2020 - Physical ailments weaken you	177
May 2020 - Light at the end of the tunnel	180
Jun 2020 - Misunderstandings detract from successes	183
Jul 2020 - Everything goes smoothly	186
Aug 2020 - Good fortune luck brings completion	189
Sep 2020 - Unexpected support brings good news	192
Oct 2020 - Energy turns foul.	195
Nov 2020 - Matters of the heart dominate	198
Dec 2020 - Keep tight leash on your short fuse	201
Jan 2021 - Feeling under the weather	204

CHAPTER

1

METAL RAT YEAR 2020
GENERAL OUTLOOK

Metal Rat Year 2020
A quarrelsome year but with hidden good luck

This year of the Metal Rat 2020 is likely to be a quarrelsome one when there will be plenty of verbal sparring between friends, and even more between foes. As a result, misunderstandings flare up more regularly than usual. It is a year that calls for more patience. Laughter is a good way to glide through the year, as humour is best way of appeasing the #7 star in the middle of the year's feng shui chart.

FENG SHUI CHART 2020

SOUTH

EARTH / DRAGON	FIRE / SNAKE / HORSE	EARTH / SHEEP
SOUTHEAST **6** Heavenly Star	**SOUTH** THREE KILLINGS **2** Illness	**SOUTHWEST** SCHOLASTIC LUCK **4** Peach Blossom
EAST WU WANG **5** Five Yellow	**CENTER** **7** BURGLARY Violence	**WEST** **9** Completion
NORTHEAST **1** Victory Luck	**NORTH** TAI SUI **3** Quarrelsome	**NORTHWEST** **8** Prosperity
EARTH / OX	WATER / RAT / PIG	EARTH / DOG

EAST — WEST

NORTH

We see many months when anger energies get doubled, which indicates that the feng shui energies of the world experience an intensity of extremes, and with the #7 star so dominant, it is a year when effort needs to be made to stay calm and collected. Do not give in to irritations and annoyances.

GOOD LEADERSHIP IN 2020

But there is good news. Because we see also that those steering the destinies of the world benefit hugely from the #8 star, which flies into the sector of the Northwest.

We can see that leaders, CEOs and all the patriarchs of the world who make decisions are less prone to succumbing to anger energies – this is because they benefit from the power of 8, which suggests good leadership skills.

This should ensure that the ship that sails in 2020 enjoys having a captain likely to enjoy excellent winds and waters. It is a year when many will benefit from stability and good governance. Patriarchs and leaders in general are likely to be calm and stable in their decision-making, thereby benefitting those who come under their leadership and influence.

IMPORTANT
TO NOT LOSE YOUR TEMPER

We need to be wary of impatience in 2020. The #7 as the dominant star number will be the cause of many succumbing to bad temper, irritation and tantrums. The feng shui chart of the year 2020 being ruled by the number 7 is indicative of violence breaking out, as a result of which the year will see a preponderance of discordant energies. The #3 star in the North meanwhile, which is in residence in the Rat sector, makes this Rat year a quarrelsome one, further suggesting that misunderstandings and conflict energies hold sway.

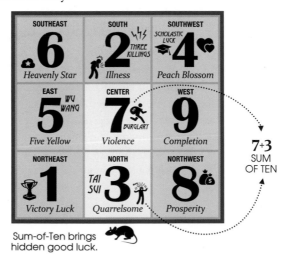

Sum-of-Ten brings hidden good luck.

HIDDEN GOOD LUCK

But... there are subtle benefits because implicit within the combination of #7 and #3 is the auspicious sum-of-ten combination. This indicates that hidden beneath misunderstandings and anger energies, a greater aspiration for harmonious completion prevails.

The SUM-OF-TEN always suggests excellent completion luck, good outcomes arising from initial intolerance and afflicted energies, suggesting that "all's well that zends well".

This is the hidden benefit of any sum-of-ten combination, when we can actually experience a bad start afflicted by misunderstanding transforming into good vibrations as a result of other factors coming in to play. Outcomes of conflict and quarrels can therefore be satisfactorily settled, with silver linings behind every cloud. There is no need to worry too much then when arguments and misunderstandings take place. Just go with the flow and let the energies play out. Things will have a way of resolving themselves.

NEW CALENDAR CYCLE

In 2020, the world gets ready to embark on a NEW calendar cycle, the start of a new 60 years, and even a new 180 years. We stand poised to welcome a NEW AGE, which we are already seeing and experiencing. The world has gone digital. We are ruled by energies that are quantum, and the strength of chi is exponentially greater as a result.

We need to expand the horizons of our aspirations and be prepared for new ideas that arise from seemingly nowhere, because creativity will also be at a new height.

Many will allow their imaginations to guide them into new directions of creativity. And because it is a Rat year, these ideas are likely to incorporate the flow of inherent prosperity which can be exploited. People on the lookout for creative new ways to grow their commercial ideas are likely to benefit from the year's energies.

> 2020 is a year when we benefit from broadening our goals to reach beyond ordinary ambitions.

This is a year when we will benefit if we indulge in "quantum thinking", which means going beyond our ordinary expectations. We must not let ourselves be boxed in. We can reach beyond space and time because at the start of this new calendar cycle, we are on the brink of many new breakthroughs.

FENG SHUI
BECOMING MORE RELEVANT

This is also a year when feng shui will become increasingly relevant, as many have now been exposed to this ancient way of looking at chi energies. The current digital age has helped disseminate this ancient knowledge to so many, and now the chi energies of the world are moving, reacting and responding at quantum speed. Thus we see energies react faster. Activities that we start will take off more quickly.

We will find that good and bad flows and accumulations of energy manifest at unprecedented speed.

Feng shui is the practice of living in harmony with the winds and waters of the world, and now these seem to be blowing faster and gathering greater strength. This correspondingly means they bring change to our luck and our well-being a lot more rapidly than before.

We are moving into an age when the winds and waters are blowing stronger and faster than ever. As we do, changes to our luck and well-being also happen more rapidly than ever before.

THE FENG SHUI CHART OF 2020

When we look at the Feng Shui Chart of 2020, we see that the dominant number in the center of the chart is 7, which is a Metal number. The element of the ruling number strengthens the energy of the WEST sector this year because METAL is the ruling element of the West.

In 2020, the element of METAL stands for wealth and financial success; thus take note that the center

SOUTHEAST	SOUTH	SOUTHWEST
6	**2** THREE KILLINGS	SCHOLASTIC LUCK **4**
Heavenly Star	*Illness*	*Peach Blossom*
EAST	CENTER	WEST
5 WU WANG	Metal Number **7**	**9**
Five Yellow	*Violence*	*Completion*
NORTHEAST	NORTH	NORTHWEST
1	TAI SUI **3**	**8**
Victory Luck	*Quarrelsome*	*Prosperity*

number being a metal number spells underlying wealth luck for the year.

MONKEY & ROOSTER BENEFIT FROM WEALTH

Note that the Monkey and Rooster reside in the West sector, hence they benefit from wealth luck due to the strength of the Metal element in the 2020 chart. These two signs can proceed to do whatever they wish to start this year, and it will be financially viable, and with success more than likely to be the result.

The Monkey and Rooster signs benefit from wealth luck in 2020.

Those married to either of these signs or having siblings of these signs can benefit by supporting them in any venture! The Monkey and Rooster are likely to initiate ventures that can create new wealth for their families.

But within the number 7 lies red, which when associated with Metal can indicate bloodshed. The year is thus likely to experience rumblings of violent energy threatening to erupt. It is beneficial thus to make extra effort to be patient and to exercise greater diplomacy in dealings with others.

SOUTHEAST	SOUTH	SOUTHWEST
6	**2**	**4**
EAST	CENTER	WEST
5	**7**	**9**
NORTHEAST	NORTH	NORTHWEST
1	**3**	**8**

4,9
HO TU

When we look at the WEST sector, we see that there is the auspicious HO TU combination of 4/9 combining SW/West. This Ho Tu brings prosperity and indicates better heads will prevail whenever anger energies threaten to erupt.

And in the sector of NW where the previous year's ferocious Dog resides, we see the benevolent and auspicious #8 star bringing lucky and auspicious energies. The #8 is also an Earth star and it is calming in its influence this year.

Note that it is the NW sector where the #8 resides, and because it brings clarity of thinking and good decision-making to this sector, the patriarchal leaders of the world are likely to benefit from this influence.

The #8 in the NW is an excellent placement indeed, manifesting good administrative capability in leaders of the world and good judgment in the patriarchal bosses within organizations and commercial corporations. More than likely then, 2020 will see growth and positive developments experienced by many people, bringing about new prosperity. This can override the unfriendly energies generated by the #7 star holding sway as the center star through the year.

A MORE STABLE YEAR

The good news is that there will be less of the upheavals of Earth and Water of previous years. In 2020, we see the sign of the Rat bringing a period of good energies that provides for sustained development. Its Water element brings stable power, and it nurtures Wood, which brings growth. There is respect for those exercising power, so law and order proceeds more smoothly in most countries.

GETTING STARTED

The main problem for many in 2020 is getting started. There are likely to be obstacles that cause delays. Problems arise that slow down the start of projects, and the transformation of ideas into action meet with hindrances. This is caused by the #7 star creating uncertainties.

THE PRESENCE OF LAP CHUN

However, the start of the lunar new year takes place on 25th January. This means there is the lap chun in 2020, which means that projects can get started smoothly. There is excellent spring luck for the year, so those wanting to initiate new undertakings can do so confident in the knowledge that this is a good year to pursue new directions. Growth is assured.

ACTIVATE THE LAP CHUN: Carry this year's specially designed **Annual Amulet 2020** which features the ruling animal sign of the year the Rat on one side with Lotus and Flowers to signify growth, and with the Rat's astrological ally the mighty Dragon on the other side shown with Ru Yi and ingots for power and wealth.

This annual amulet symbolises you benefitting fully from the presence of the Lap Chun this year while staying protected against the worst of its afflictions.

MONEY TO BE MADE

The prospects for the global economy are promising. There will be sufficient resources and new wealth can get created. There is enough prosperity to make many people happy. There is money to be made. In fact, for those who are able to tap into personal veins of good fortune, 2020 can turn out to be a breakout year indeed.

This is a promise of the Rat Year, which is always a great year to create new wealth. The Rat is the sign that is famous for having the capability to eke out prosperity from very minimal resources.

Rat years are always years when money can be made! Display the Wealth Mongoose Spouting Jewels in the NW this year.

This Rat Year has some afflictions that need to be neutralized.

Unfortunately in 2020, the Rat sector of the NORTH plays host to the TAI SUI and it also faces the energy of the Three Killings. This double affliction directly facing the Rat's sector of North brings distractions and unfortunate obstacles – big and small. Many of these problems will arise from small-mindedness, manifesting as problems within interpersonal relationships. It causes people to get sidetracked and distracted. This is a year when it is a challenge to stay focused.

OUTLOOK FOR THE 12 ANIMALS

The **ROOSTER** enjoys the promise of great good fortune, brought by the stars of *Big Auspicious* in the 24 Mountains compass of 2020. How much of this good luck potential can materialize will depend on this sign's creativity and intelligence. But with the #9 star in its sector, there is excellent completion luck. The Rooster gets stronger this year and continues on from the previous year's fast pace of activities.

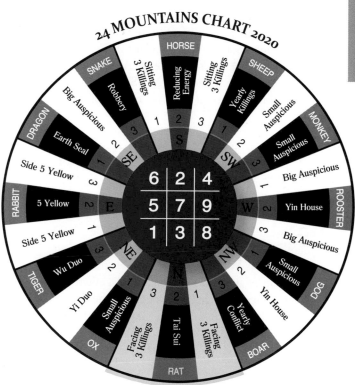

24 MOUNTAINS CHART 2020

24 Mountains Compass of 2020 and its influence on the luck of the 12 animal signs

23

But there is a *Star of Yin House* sitting in its sector and this suggests the possibility of there being the loss of someone close. Subdue bad vibes of this *Yin House Star* by displaying the **Yang Energy Amulet** in the West corner of the home. It is MOST important to suppress this affliction if there are old people living in the home.

Two other animal signs enjoying *Big Auspicious* are those born in the years of the **DRAGON** and **SNAKE**. For these two signs, heaven luck shines bright, so there are unexpected windfalls coming their way. It is a good idea to enhance with a **Heaven Luck Enhancing Mirror** for this incredible good luck to manifest. Carrying good luck charms that bring success such as **Windhorse hangings** is the way to go for this pair of signs this year. It is an excellent idea for both Dragon and Snake to energize the *Star of Big Auspicious* that lies between their sectors in the SE by placing the **Treasure Chest Dharani** in the SE of the home to attract good fortune energy.

The Dragon also enjoys the luck of the *Earth Seal,* which brings excellent grounding luck, but for the Snake, good fortune indications gets clouded by the danger of getting robbed this year. The Snake must make certain to carry the **Anti-Robbery Amulet** this year. The Dragon must carry or display the **Earth Seal**

Amulet to ensure its intrinsic Earth element does not get diluted this year.

In 2020, the sign of the East is afflicted by the *Five Yellow* and hence requires the help of the **Five Element Pagoda**. The sign of the **RABBIT** must watch that the bad luck brought by this afflictive star does not bring mischief its way. The Rabbit definitely needs to display the Five Element Pagoda cure prominently in its sector to subdue all the bad luck vibrations brought by the *wu wang* star of #5. In 2020, the Rabbit should watch its back, as it is likely to suffer the consequences of some old grievance surfacing that could cause plenty of worry and trouble.

The **SHEEP** sits on the *Star of Yearly Killings*, a minor afflictive star, but its sector mate the **MONKEY** brings a double dose of auspicious energy from *Small Auspicious stars* that bring good energy in small doses through the year. The Sheep must subdue the "killing" energy and enhance the auspicious chi coming from the direction of the Monkey. The best way to do this is to place a **Bejewelled Reflecting Mirror** facing towards the Monkey and Rooster directions (i.e. the SW and West).

The **MONKEY** in 2020 is on a roll and should have no problem staying ahead of the competition, especially those working in professional careers or competing for high honours of some kind. It sits on and is flanked by *Small and Big Auspicious* stars in 2020. Those doing business get assistance easily and those still at school will find the year bringing many small and big successes. This sign should however be careful not to get distracted by romantic inclinations. It benefits to stay cool and detached this year.

The **TIGER** will have a relatively quiet year, while the **OX** sits on a *Star of Small Auspicious*. This is a year of many small victories brought by the Victory Star 1 in their sector. This year, it is a good idea to place victory-enhancing and other **success symbols** in the NE sector. Using *Art of Placement* feng shui benefits these two signs. Thus display the **Windhorse-Boosting Victory Flag** and the powerful **Red Windhorse** in the Northeast to attract success luck for both signs.

The **RAT** and **HORSE** should work at generating good energy and strengthening themselves in 2020. The Rat plays host to the *TAI SUI* who is the God of the Year (a very good thing), while the Horse sits on the *Star of Reducing Energy*. Both signs face their respective challenges in 2020 and are in need of help from powerful energizing Deities such as **Kuan Kung** or the **Four Heavenly Kings**.

Those who understand the role of symbolic placement power in feng shui know that the mere presence of these Taoist Deities radiate good fortune vibes wherever they are placed, but especially when there are afflictive stars present. It is for this reason that these Taoist deities have retained their huge popularity through the centuries. Even until today, you can see their images on many decorative display items in homes across China, and in Chinese homes all round the world.

Four Heavenly Kings

The **BOAR** and **DOG** enjoy the magical sign of 8 in 2020. The Dog also has a *Small Auspicious Star* so that the year brings many small victories. The Boar however must contend with the *Yearly Conflict Star* and is well advised to refrain from getting into arguments with others.

CHAPTER

2

FOUR PILLARS CHART 2020

FOUR PILLARS CHART 2020

HOUR	DAY	MONTH	YEAR
己	丁	戊	庚
Yin Earth	Yin Fire	Yang Earth	Yang Metal
辛 酉	己 丑	甲 寅	壬 子
Yin Metal Rooster	Yin Earth Ox	Yang Wood Tiger	Yang Water Rat

THE YEAR'S FOUR PILLARS

To get an overall feel for the destiny outlook of the year, we must analyze the year's Four Pillars chart. This reveals the impact of the five elements interacting with the animal signs in the year's chart. The various combinations within the chart offer insights into what's in store. Thus we take a look at the eight elements dominating the Four Pillars of the year's Paht Chee. We look at the way the heavenly stems and earthly branches combine together, and further examine the luck pillars of the 12 months of the year.

29

The 2020 Paht Chee chart reveals a year when all five elements are present. This indicates a well-balanced year where nothing is missing.

EARTH BRINGS CREATIVITY

There is dominance of EARTH energy, but the ruling element is weak YIN fire. This will be a harmonious year when good sense and logical minds exert a big influence, so there should not be any very major conflicts, and focus will be on the search for knowledge. 2020 is a year when a renewed respect rises for those with creativity and intelligence. It will be an extremely beneficial year for those seeking knowledge.

HOUR	DAY	MONTH	YEAR
己	丁	戊	庚
Yin **Earth**	Yin Fire	Yang **Earth**	Yang Metal
辛 酉	己 丑	甲 寅	壬 子
Yin Metal Rooster	Yin **Earth** Ox	Yang Wood Tiger	Yang Water Rat

The 2020 Paht Chee chart is dominated by **Earth**, which represents intelligence and creativity this year.

NO MISSING ELEMENTS

A quick glance at the Paht Chee chart reveals all five elements are present, implying there is no imbalance of energies. We also see that the YEAR Pillar has Metal PRODUCING Water, and in the DAY Pillar, Fire is PRODUCING Earth. These are the two most important pillars, and with the elements in a productive relationship, there is favourable indication of excellent productivity. There is hence a productive yin and a productive yang pillar in the chart.

	"Productive"		*"Productive"*
HOUR	**DAY**	**MONTH**	**YEAR**
己	丁	戊	庚
Yin Earth	Yin Fire	Yang Earth	Yang Metal
辛 酉	己 丑	甲 寅	壬 子
Yin Metal Rooster	Yin Earth Ox	Yang Wood Tiger	Yang Water Rat

The two most important pillars - the **Year Pillar** and the **Day Pillar** - are both in productive relationship, one being Yang in nature, the other Yin.

31

RELATIONSHIPS GET A BOOST

Rooster and Ox in the HOUR and DAY pillars are indication of good rapport between parents and children. Good sense prevails in the bringing up of children this year. Relationships between spouses are harmonious as indicated by the productive elements. Here, Fire produces Earth, indicating greater domestic harmony in 2020.

Rat and Ox in the YEAR and DAY pillars are further indication that despite the discordant #7 in the center of the year's Flying Star chart, relationships will stay resilient despite temporary difficulties.

HOUR	DAY	MONTH	YEAR
己	丁	戊	庚
Yin Earth	Yin Fire	Yang Earth	Yang Metal
辛 酉	己 丑	甲 寅	壬 子
Yin Metal **Rooster**	Yin Earth **Ox**	Yang Wood Tiger	Yang Water Rat

Allies

Secret Friend/Soulmate Combination

The **Rooster** and **Ox** in the Hour and Day Pillars suggest excellent rapport between parents and children in 2020, while the **Rat** and **Ox** in the Year and Day Pillars point to long term bonds reigning supreme over short term conflicts.

Rat and Ox are secret friends and soulmates of the zodiac, and the presence of this combination in the Earthly branches suggest that while on the surface things may be challenging, good sense will ultimately prevail. Bridges do not get burned over petty, inconsequential matters.

Rat Years are years when opportunities for enhancing family prosperity motivates the younger members of the family to think up wonderful new ideas.

It is advisable never to dismiss fresh ideas offered by the younger members of the family. The world is evolving, and increasingly, our "young ones" are bringing invaluable new perspectives to the way we live, work and enjoy life.

WEALTH LUCK
BROUGHT BY METAL ELEMENT

The Metal Rat Year is a pacifying year filled with many prosperity opportunities. It benefits to view the year positively, as the coming twelve months from February 4th 2020 till February 4th 2021 will see many fresh new opportunities for creating wealth. It is beneficial to live in a state of awareness, being totally mindful to new

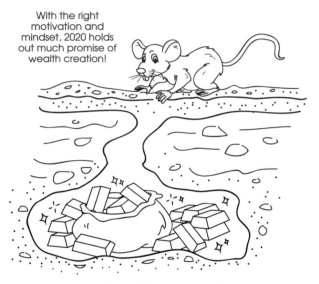

With the right motivation and mindset, 2020 holds out much promise of wealth creation!

avenues for growth and development. This is a year when being creative reaps dividends.

There is wealth luck available to be tapped. What is needed is a keen eye and the motivation to get started and to take action. Think outside the box and look for new ways of producing, packaging and marketing goods and services.

The global business scenario has been changing fast in the past decade. Breakthrough technology and applications bring many prominent players into the technology game. The good news is that anyone can take fullest advantage of the global scenario for commerce to flourish in the digital and internet age.

We have been living in the Period of 8 which has favoured China, but the Period of 9 is coming, and it is a great idea for anyone looking to the longer term future and keen on building their businesses to start looking SOUTH, as this is the coming of the Period of 9 and energy strength is pointing us to this direction for new expansion and growth chances.

As we enter the last quarter of Period 8 and approach the Period of 9, global growth opportunities are likely to change.

HIDDEN STARS OF 2020

A very positive aspect of the coming year is the appearance of three extremely lucky stars - the *Star of Scholastic Brilliance*, the *Commanding Star* and the *Star of Powerful Mentors*. These hidden stars are brought by the year's Paht Chee, and what they suggest are the potential for new inventions, new innovations and exciting new directions in business and commerce, and also in personal endeavours.

STAR OF
SCHOLASTIC
BRILLIANCE

COMMANDING
STAR

STAR OF
POWERFUL
MENTORS

On a macro level, the world will likely see a further shift to an even more digitalized age, led by the brilliant young minds of tomorrow. On a personal level, all three stars indicate the presence of superior intellect, superior mentors and guidance, and the self-motivation to pursue excellence in whatever one may be engaged in. There is likely to be unprecedented originality of thought, advancing our existence in multiple directions. There will continue to be huge leaps and advances in the way we work, the way we play and the way we live.

Money will no longer be made through conventional means. Those who make it big will be those who can spot windows of opportunity and who go after these with speed and gusto.

ACTIVATION IS NEEDED!

The most important thing to remember when you read this book is that in Chinese Destiny Analysis, we do not hold the Western view that one's destiny is set in stone. Indeed, the Four Pillars chart is not a "prediction"; it is a road map to success which can be followed to profit from the myriad opportunities presented by the year.

To the Chinese, for good fortune to manifest, one has to infuse each one of these indications with *yang* energy. One has to breathe *life* into them.

The lucky indications of the year must be activated for their effects to be felt. This should be done both with self-effort as well as the placement of the correct symbols and enhancers, if one is to enjoy its benefits to the fullest.

1 *STAR OF SCHOLASTIC BRILLIANCE enhances the power of scholarship*

This star makes an appearance again in this year's chart, indicating that scholarship and academic excellence continues to open doors to the best jobs and the best opportunities. Those with scholastic honours and accolades to their names continue to impress and the benefits of their qualifications go beyond the knowledge and skills acquired during their courses of study.

The *Scholastic Brilliance Star* of 2020 gets formed by the year's self element of YIN FIRE with the ROOSTER in the Hour Pillar.

HOUR	DAY	MONTH	YEAR
己 Yin Earth	丁 Yin Fire	戊 Yang Earth	庚 Yang Metal
辛 酉 Yin Metal Rooster	己 丑 Yin Earth Ox	甲 寅 Yang Wood Tiger	壬 子 Yang Water Rat

The **Star of Scholastic Brilliance** brings success to those pursuing knowledge & scholastic endeavours.

Of all the twelve signs, the Rooster is the most akin to paying meticulous attention to detail. Together with its natural flair for pomp and pageantry, this indicates that success in academic endeavours will come to those who combine resilient hard work with the ability to demonstrate that work at the right time.

The Yin Fire indicates that it will be those capable of short sharp spurts of brilliance who will get noticed rather than the solid workhorse who ploughs through slow and steady. This is not to say that consistent good work is unimportant, only that this year, those who rise to the fore to shine will be those who make it a part of their plan to shine at the right time.

Fire is an element that is bright and brilliant, but it is also an element that requires fuel to sustain it. Similarly, to achieve scholastic brilliance this year will require the continued drive and motivation to succeed, coupled with attention to detail when it counts the most - exam time. That it is Yin Fire (rather than Yang) re-emphasizes the need for the stamina to stay the course, simmering and smoldering with periods of brilliant fire.

To activate this year's *Scholastic Brilliance Star*, we suggest the **13-level Bejewelled Wisdom Pagoda** in bright red. This pagoda not only epitomizes examination and scholastic success for children, it also empowers the young adult looking to make a name for him or herself in the working world.

Containing the most precious *Treasure Chest Dharani* sutra, placed on the workdesk, it empowers you with countless blessings to excel in all your endeavours. You can also place it in the SW which houses the Scholastic Star of the year, or the West, which is flanked by two stars of Big Auspicious.

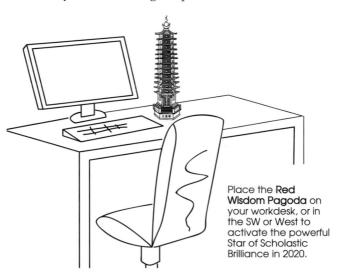

Place the **Red Wisdom Pagoda** on your workdesk, or in the SW or West to activate the powerful Star of Scholastic Brilliance in 2020.

2 *COMMANDING STAR brings benevolent leaders*

The outstandingly auspicious Commanding Star is formed by the combination of the OX in the Day Pillar with the ROOSTER in the Hour Pillar.

This set of allies from the Trinity of Intellectuals suggests that power and influence lies with superior mindpower. It will be intellect that is admired and revered, and that will provide leaders with what they need to lead. Leaders, bosses and anyone in a position of command will find it far more effective to lead with brains than with brawn this year.

HOUR	DAY	MONTH	YEAR
己	丁	戊	庚
Yin Earth	Yin Fire	Yang Earth	Yang Metal
辛 酉	己 丑	甲 寅	壬 子
Yin Metal Rooster	Yin Earth Ox	Yang Wood Tiger	Yang Water Rat

The **Commanding Star** brings authority and influence luck, benefitting those in positions of authority.

41

The appearance of this star together with the powerful #8 in the NW, the sector of the leader, suggests 2020 will bring wise and benevolent leadership at all levels.

> The Commanding Star brings authority, power and influence luck to the year, benefitting those who find themselves in positions of authority.

Indeed the year benefits those who know how to use their influence and power, so managers with a clear idea of their strategy or focus will benefit especially from this star. Leaders will find the energy of the year increases their effectiveness, and the mantle of leadership comes easily for them.

FENG SHUI ENHANCER: To activate the luck of the Commanding Star, display the **Jade Emperor Heaven Amulet** in a prominent place in the Northwest of your home or living room, or on your office or study desk where you work.

If you hold a CEO, managerial or leadership position at work, you should also have the **Three Warriors - Zhang Fei, Kuan Kung and Liu Bei** in your office. These are the three great heroes of Chinese history, who personify courage, integrity and honour. They symbolize success achieved through clever strategy and effective diplomacy; beating the competition without having to resort to undesirable or underhanded tactics.

Anyone in a position of leadership should have the Three Warriors Liu Bei, Kuan Kung and Zhang Fei in their office. They are the best way to empower the Commanding Star of the year for effective leadership and influence.

3 STAR OF POWERFUL MENTORS
brings support of influential people

This star is brought by the OX in the Day Pillar and the Heavenly Stem of YANG METAL in the Year Pillar. This year's *Star of Powerful Mentors* suggests that for the younger generation determined to succeed, the year will be filled with influential people turning up in their lives to give them strong, meaningful and powerful support.

HOUR	DAY	MONTH	YEAR
己	丁	戊	庚
Yin Earth	Yin Fire	Yang Earth	Yang Metal
辛 酉	己 丑	甲 寅	壬 子
Yin Metal Rooster	Yin Earth Ox	Yang Wood Tiger	Yang Water Rat

The **Star of Powerful Mentors** brings support from powerful and influential people.

The presence of this star is a reminder to heed the advice of those in the generation above you. Although much of the action this year will involve the youth and younger generation, the older folk will have plenty of influence in the background.

The animal signs that stand to gain most from the *Star of Powerful Mentors* in 2020 are the **Dragon, Snake, Rooster** and **Rat**.

These signs, and all other signs, should activate this star by displaying the **9-Dragon Kuan Kung** facing the front door of the home. You can also display Kuan Kung behind you at your desk for support from important people in a position to help you.

Display the 9-Dragon Kuan Kung in the vicinity of your main door to activate Star of Powerful Mentors.

IMPORTANCE OF A STRONG LIFE FORCE

Whatever a year holds in store, to benefit fully from the auspicious indications on offer, one has to have sufficient Life Force. This year, those benefitting from excellent levels of Life Force continue to be the WOOD signs of **Tiger** and **Rabbit,** while the EARTH signs of **Ox, Dragon, Sheep** and **Dog** continue to enjoy very good levels. For these six signs, you are blessed with the ability to turn ideas into reality. You are constantly filled with an inner drive, which keeps you resolute and very action-oriented. You enjoy a strong self-conviction and will not be easily flustered or swayed.

The Wood signs of Tiger and Rabbit, and the Earth signs of Ox, Dragon, Sheep and Dog enjoy excellent levels of Life Force, allowing them to make the most of the exciting opportunities brought by the 2020 chart.

The WATER signs of **Rat** and **Boar** have good levels of Life Force, while the METAL signs of **Monkey** and **Rooster** have neutral levels.

The FIRE signs of **Snake** and **Horse** continue to suffer from very poor levels of Life Force. Both Snake and Horse thus MUST make every effort to increase their personal Life Force levels or they could find themselves succumbing to defeat before they even get started.

FENG SHUI CURE: Carry the **Windhorse with Life Force Amulet** at all times, and constantly work at building up self-confidence and self-esteem.

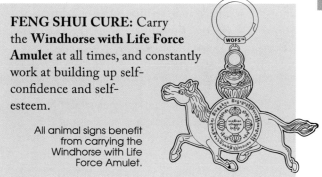

All animal signs benefit from carrying the Windhorse with Life Force Amulet.

Both Snake and Horse need to be especially watchful of the company they keep. Surrounding oneself with "friends" who make you feel inferior or inadequate is the surest way of ensuring you fail to overcome the year's afflictions.

STRENGTHENING
SUCCESS LUCK in 2020

While all the ingredients are there for the coming Rat Year to be good one, this can only be done with sufficient *Lung Ta* levels. When your personal *lung ta* or Windhorse is weak, no matter how hard you try or what strings you manage to pull, success will prove elusive.

What everyone should do as a matter of course each year is to raise their Windhorse energies. This should be done at the start of the year and also regularly throughout the year.

In 2020, the three signs that enjoy excellent success luck are the *Trinity of Diplomats* comprising the **Rabbit, Sheep** and **Boar**. For these signs, the advice is to go for it, whatever it is they may be aspiring to or wishing for. Luck is strongly on your side and everything you put your focus on succeeds easily, with results coming quickly. The *Trinity of Adventurers* made up of **Dog, Horse** and **Tiger** also have good levels of *lung ta* in 2020. These signs too can proceed with confidence in whatever they set their minds to.

But the *Trinity of Intellectuals* comprising **Snake, Rooster** and **Ox,** and the *Trinity of Competitors* made up of **Rat, Dragon** and **Monkey** have neutral and bad levels of *lung ta* respectively, so for them, we strongly suggest carrying **Windhorse amulets** to boost their potential for success.

The best way to boost one's success luck for the year is to carry the Windhorse as a portable amulet and display a prominent Windhorse within sight of your workdesk.

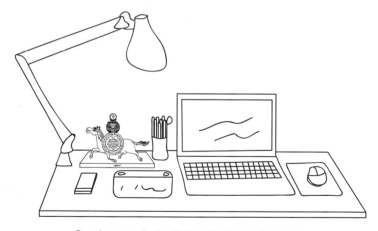

Boost success luck with the Windhorse. Especially needed in 2020 for Snake, Rooster, Ox, Rat, Dragon and Monkey.

Releasing Windhorse balloons is an excellent way to raise one's potential for success. Great to do at the start of the year.

It is also incredibly effective to regularly perform Windhorse balloon rituals (we print the Windhorse mantras on five-element coloured balloons and these are made available for purchase on *www.fsmegamall.com* for those who would like to perform this ritual.)

Once a month - or more regularly if you like - fill Windhorse balloons with helium and display them for at least one full day. Make sure you have one balloon in each of the five colours of RED, WHITE, BLUE, YELLOW and GREEN as you recite the Windhorse mantra while making a heartfelt wish.

The Windhorse Mantra:
KI KI SO SO LAJA LO

LUCK OF THE RAT IN 2020

*Rat Enjoys Support of
Tai Sui in 2020*

ELEMENT LUCK OF THE

RAT 2020	YEAR ELEMENT	FIRE RAT 84/24 Years	EARTH RAT 72/12 Years
LIFE FORCE	WATER	Good O	Good O
HEALTH	EARTH	Very Bad XX	Neutral OX
WEALTH	METAL	Very Good OO	Neutral OX
SUCCESS (Lung Ta)	WOOD	Bad X	Bad X
SPIRIT ESSENCE	METAL	Bad X	Bad X

RAT 2020

METAL RAT *60 Years*	WATER RAT *48 Years*	WOOD RAT *36 Years*
Good O	Good O	Good O
Good O	Very Good OO	Excellent OOO 👍
Bad X	Excellent OOO 👍	Very Bad XX
Bad X	Bad X	Bad X
Bad X	Bad X	Bad X

ELEMENT LUCK OF THE RAT IN 2020

The chart in the previous spread shows how your personal elements of the year interact with those of the year 2020 in five important luck categories.

A key indicator is the success indicator, which affects all Rats equally and unfortunately, this year's success luck looks uninspiring; indeed, it is indicating that it is better not to take risks this year, as it looks weak. This, coupled with a weak level of spirit essence is advising Rats to not take risks and not go out on a limb for anyone. This year's astrological advice is to stay low-key.

The Rat's element luck in 2020 enters a mixed year. Your sign has good life force but weak spirit essence, which suggests you are likely to feel disoriented through the year.

It seems as if you are uncertain of outcomes each time you make a significant decision that impacts on your work. There also tend to be uncertainties in your personal life. Thus, while your vitality and attitude towards work and personal matters appear stable on the surface, you have self-doubts that affect your levels of confidence. Be aware of your uncertainties, and acknowledge them to stabilize your attitudes this year. If you dismiss your self-doubts without dealing with them, you will feel even more unsettled. This is how people get set on a downward spiral that affects their confidence.

Your element luck in 2020 show good life force but weak spirit essence and this means that while on the surface you come across self-assured and strong, inside, you have pockets of uncertainty about your abilities.

In short, this year, all those born under the sign of the Rat lack their usual self-confidence. Perhaps something happens early in the year that shakes this confidence – a betrayal, a disappointment or even a downright bad turn of events that upsets your sense of stability. Whatever it is, dig in your heels and stay strong.

The Rat is saddled with the #3 star and this brings about a work environment that is hostile and a home environment that is quarrelsome. If you have placed the cures to suppress the #3 and still feel the negative hostile energies, then **wear red** more often and place a double dose of **Fire energy** (lights, the colour red and a pair of red Pi Yaos) in your living space where you spend the most time.

In 2020, the symbol of the **Red Windhorse** is a must have. Place this mighty red steed anywhere on your desk and instantly your success *lung ta* gets activated. This powerful symbol of success will help suppress the negatives that obstruct your success luck.

The other thing you need to do is to use element therapy to improve your spirit essence. This luck category suggests that your inner strength is weak. Boost your spirit essence by placing **Earth element energizers** in the North. You can also carry the **Spirit Essence Enhancing Amulet**. Note that when our spirit essence is strong, everything about us is strong, but when it is weak, we tend to give up easily, making it harder to stay focused this year. So you need to be your own motivator.

It is a good thing your life force is at a good level – as this suggests that at least your level of vitality is strong. Some years we are more active than in other years, and this is reflected in a good life force.

Vitality is an indication of how strong our minds are. This helps sustain our inner confidence levels. What you need is to suppress any self-doubts you may harbour. This affliction causes you to hesitate each time you want to move forward.

ENHANCE EARTH ELEMENT ENERGY

Place **crystals** in your personal space and wear **big gemstones** through the year. Gemstones are concentrated vortexes of Earth energy; wear them touching your skin. The Earth element strengthens the Rat's Spirit Essence levels in a year when your spirit essense is weak.

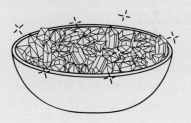

As for the Rat's life force, it is at a good level, but if you can stay calm and focused on making good strategic moves in all aspects of your life, the year has much greater potential to turn out well for you.

EARTH RAT 12 Years	
LIFE FORCE	GOOD
HEALTH	NEUTRAL
WEALTH	NEUTRAL
SUCCESS (Lung Ta)	BAD
SPIRIT ESSENCE	BAD

The **12 year old Earth Rat** has the vitality to move ahead this year. Enjoy your coming-of-age year and make strong resolutions to forge ahead in your school life. This is a year you can work on building confidence in areas you have specific interests in. Try your hand at new things and don't enter with any pre-conceived ideas. Results may not come immediately so you should take a more long-term approach when making plans. Commitment and dedication pays off.

RAISE YOUR WINDHORSE: The **12 year old Rat** benefits from boosting its personal *lung ta* this year. While the year ahead holds a lot of promise for you, to fulfil your true potential, you could use the help of King Gesar's magical steed the **Red Windhorse**. Carry the **Windhorse Amulet**. Clip onto your schoolbag. Your luckiest colour this year is blue. Wear this colour to give your inner sense a boost. This will help you rediscover the self-confidence you need to continually set meaningful goals for yourself.

FIRE RAT 24 Years	
LIFE FORCE	GOOD
HEALTH	VERY BAD
WEALTH	VERY GOOD
SUCCESS (Lung Ta)	BAD
SPIRIT ESSENCE	BAD

The **24 year old Fire Rat** enjoys very good wealth luck and should be laying the groundwork for creating prosperity for the years to come. Add **Wood energy** to your desk to energize the brightness of your wealth luck, as your good life force gives you the strength to move ahead. Young Rats starting out in their careers can use this as a preparation year to keep building on the new skills you are acquiring.

GOOD WEALTH POOR HEALTH: While the **24 year old Rat** is doing well financially, there are dangers associated with exhaustion, burn-out or simply succumbing to illness. Keep the **Wu Lou Garuda Health Amulet** with you. Carry the **Blue Mantra Wand** filled with Medicine Buddha's mantras. Be mindful when your body is telling you to slow down and take things a little more easy.

WOOD RAT 36 Years	
LIFE FORCE	GOOD
HEALTH	EXCELLENT
WEALTH	VERY BAD
SUCCESS (Lung Ta)	BAD
SPIRIT ESSENCE	BAD

The **36 year old Wood Rat** is in the same boat as the older Rat in that you have the vitality to act on new ideas and fresh opportunities but unlike the other Rats, your wealth luck is weak. This is not the year to gamble or to take big risks that are likely to compromise your financial situation. Err on the side of caution. You are feeling however physically strong; make use of your mental clarity and your physical strength to keep making good strides in whatever you are pursuing.

AVOID TAKING FINANCIAL RISKS: Money luck is not promising for the 36 year old Rat. Do not take big risks when it comes to money. Do not gamble or speculate. Carry the **Wealth Mongoose Amulet** to give your wealth element luck a boost. Carry your cash in the **Mongoose Wealth Wallet**.

WATER RAT 48 Years	
LIFE FORCE	GOOD
HEALTH	VERY GOOD
WEALTH	EXCELLENT
SUCCESS (Lung Ta)	BAD
SPIRIT ESSENCE	BAD

The **48 year old Water Rat** is especially lucky this year. But like all Rat signs you lack the determination to put in extra effort simply because you are lacking in self-confidence this year. But your wealth luck is strong and you possess really good financial luck. You can pursue new directions in business and investments with confidence; if you spot a good opportunity, don't let fear of the unknown hold you back. Allow yourself to dream big enough. You have solid element luck backing you, so if you have a good feeling about something, by all means you should go for it.

BOOST SPIRIT ESSENCE: The **48 year old Rat** has most things going for you but you lack the confidence to stand  by your own instincts. Carry the **Spirit Essence Enhancing Amulet**. Wear the **Wealth & Wisdom Ring** to guide you to make all the right decisions and at the right time.

METAL RAT 60 Years	
LIFE FORCE	GOOD
HEALTH	GOOD
WEALTH	BAD
SUCCESS (Lung Ta)	BAD
SPIRIT ESSENCE	BAD

The **60 year old Metal Rat** enjoys good health and good life force. This is a year to enjoy life. Go for a vacation and spend time with loved ones. Wealth luck is not as promising, so avoid taking financial risks or making new investments. Personal pursuits go better for this Rat than work-related and financial ones. Spend more time nurturing yourself spiritually.

GROW YOUR WEALTH: The **60 year old Rat** needs to pursue steady ways to expand your wealth and avoid risky investments as your wealth element luck is very weak. Have the **5 Rats Attracting Jar** in the home and fill it with goodies,  small change, cash, ingots, anything that represents wealth to you. You are at an age where you should think beyond just making money and in this year when your financial luck is weak, don't go looking to make the quick buck. You can expand your asset wealth with blue chip investments but anything that carries risk is bad news.

EARTH RAT 72 Years	
LIFE FORCE	GOOD
HEALTH	NEUTRAL
WEALTH	NEUTRAL
SUCCESS (Lung Ta)	BAD
SPIRIT ESSENCE	BAD

The **72 year old Earth Rat** needs to work harder than other Rat signs to enjoy good health. Keep your rooms well-lit and spend time in gardens breathing in Wood energies. These will help you breathe life back into your bones and keep you strong in a somewhat afflicted year.

Take things more easily when it comes to your responsibilities. This is an age when if you are still working, you should think about slowing down. This does not mean to stop doing things altogether, but your should avoid activities that cause you to worry or feel stressed out. Learn to enjoy life, treat yourself to nice things and holidays with your family and loved ones. Don't take your health for granted. Watch your diet and maintain some gentle exercise daily.

SYMBOLS OF LONGEVITY:
The **72 year old Rat** benefits from displaying **Sau, the God of Longevity** in the home. Let him bring in the energies of good health, long life and a harmonious home atmosphere. You can also invite in **White Tara**,

the Goddess of Longevity, known to ease suffering from sickness, poor health and age-related ailments. Place on your altar or on a respectful high table or sideboard. You can also carry **Medicine Buddha's Mantra Wand** to invoke his curative blessings and to wave away health obstacles brought by your element luck indications. Don't get crotchety with the younger generation. Conflict and arguments, usually overly mundane and unimportant matters, will only get your blood pressure up and is bad for you. Work at enjoying all that life has to offer, and sometimes all that is needed is a shift in attitude. If you learn to be more relaxed, you will enjoy yourself a lot more.

FIRE RAT 84 Years	
LIFE FORCE	GOOD
HEALTH	VERY BAD
WEALTH	VERY GOOD
SUCCESS *(Lung Ta)*	BAD
SPIRIT ESSENCE	BAD

The **84 year old Fire Rat** enjoys very good wealth luck. You can enhance your net worth! But take care of your health. Don't ignore ailments however minor.

At your age, you need to look after yourself. Don't exert yourself too much and know your limits. Give yourself enough rest each day and limit your indulgence of rich foods. Your mind is still active but your physical limits may frustrate you. Engage in things that challenge the mind, but you may have to give up on some of your more physical passions. The year can be a very happy one for this Rat, as long as you don't let yourself get worried or stressed out over things that don't matter. The more easy going you can learn to be, the happier the year will be for you.

LOOK AFTER YOUR HEALTH: The **84 year old Rat** needs to be concerned with only one thing this year, and it is to stay healthy. Avoid stressful situations, don't work your blood pressure up by holding on to dogmatic views, learn to agree to disagree. Place the **White Tara Gau Home Amulet** in your home sector of North, and invite the **God of Longevity Sau** in the home. These are auspicious symbols of good health and long life and will help keep you shielded from harmful health obstacles.

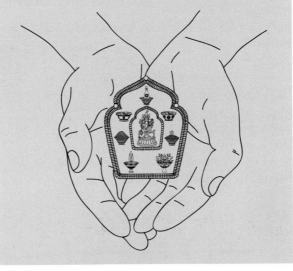

CHAPTER

4

FLYING STAR CHART OF 2020

FLYING STAR CHART OF 2020
Energies of loss & betrayal need to be subdued

The feng shui chart of the year which lays out the location of the year's flying stars in 2020 is dominated by the energy of 7, a troublesome star which can bring problems; it is the reigning number of this year's chart and its effects must be respected. More importantly, in any household, its impact must be subdued.

The 2020 chart is dominated by the violent star 7, which gets exacerbated by the 3 in the home sector of the animal sign of the year, the Rat.

The number 7 is a Metal number that represents the harmful side of relationships, symbolizing treachery, loss and betrayal.

More importantly, the number is strengthened by the Earth energy of the center grid, so the negative energies it releases - that of hostility that leads to quarrels - must be kept under control.

Unfortunately, this year's animal sign of the Rat brings the Quarrelsome Star #3 into play. Here the number is located in the NORTH and because it is dominant this year, the #3 star aggravates the discordant vibrations of the year. This can cause the year's overriding energies to be hostile and suspicious.

Thus in spite of there being a good balance of elements in the year's Paht Chee, 2020 will nevertheless see a tendency towards confrontation. There is likely to be continued violence, both on the world stage as well as within countries and within household and individual situations.

It is thus judicious to always be careful and to play safe rather than be affected. Treat the #7 star in the center with respect and actively subdue with feng shui cures and element antidotes.

This is a year when trickery and scheming are likely to occur more frequently than usual. This is brought about by a higher occurrence of betrayals and by the unbridled aggressiveness of ambitious people.

2020 is a year when the CENTER of buildings, houses and offices benefit from the presence of Water to subdue the strength of the #7 star.

Luckily, the 7 is a weak star in the current Period of 8, so it is easier to subdue. We are nevertheless nearing the end of Period of 8, with just 4 years remaining, so we need to keep in mind that the number 7 is re-strengthening. It is getting stronger even as we get nearer to Period 9.

Anything of a **black or dark blue colour** can work well at keeping the #7 under control. But it is advisable to make a concerted effort to do so in all homes and offices. This protects residents from becoming victims of unfair politicking and guard against troublemakers at the workplace.

This year, activate the CENTER of the home with WATER energy, and place the Blue Rhino and Elephant with Anti-Burglary Talisman here.

In 2020, activate the **power of Water** in the home. Invest in a **small water feature** to create the presence of moving water in the CENTER grid of the home. You should also place the **Blue Rhino and Elephant with the Anti-Burglary Talisman** to suppress the negative influence of 7.

The luck of the different sectors of any abode is influenced by new energy brought by the year's feng shui chart. This chart reveals the year's auspicious and inauspicious sectors for all buildings, houses and apartments, and for individual rooms within buildings and homes.

LO SHU SQUARE

SOUTHEAST	SOUTH	SOUTHWEST
4	**9**	**2**
EAST	**CENTER**	**WEST**
3	**5**	**7**
NORTHEAST	**NORTH**	**NORTHWEST**
8	**1**	**6**

FLYING STAR CHART OF 2020

SOUTHEAST	SOUTH	SOUTHWEST
6	**2**	**4**
EAST	**CENTER**	**WEST**
5	**7**	**9**
NORTHEAST	**NORTH**	**NORTHWEST**
1	**3**	**8**

On the left is the original Lo Shu chart. The right shows 2020's chart. At the start of each year, one of the most important things you must do is to take note of the new annual placement of the stars, and enhance and remedy each sector as needed.

The chart for 2020 reveals the different numbers in each of the nine grids in this 3x3 sector chart. This looks like the original Lo Shu square which reveals the role of numbers in time dimension feng shui. In each year, the numbers placed in each grid change according to the center number. With 7 in the center, the other numbers in the other eight sectors of the chart are then placed around the grid sectors. The sequence of placing the numbers follow the original Lo Shu flying star pattern and with each number bringing different kinds of luck to the different compass sectors; the luck of the different sectors can be analyzed and dealt with.

This is what updating the feng shui of homes or office buildings means. Doing so correctly ensures good feng shui for the next twelve months.

The numbers that "fly" into each sector brings significant transformations to the "luck outlook" not just of rooms located in the sectors; they also affect the luck of each of the animal signs, arising from the fact that each of the 12 signs occupies a particular compass sector influenced by each number.

The **RAT person** occupies the North sector in the feng shui chart and we can see that in the 2020 chart those born under this sign of the Rat are affected by the number 3, which signifies quarrels and misunderstandings. Thus in 2020, those born under the Rat sign are likely to be less tolerant than usual. It is necessary to make an extra effort at anger management and at keeping your temper in check.

But also note that the #3 of the NORTH and the #7 of the center form the productive *sum-of-ten* combination. This brings *Completion Luck* and can be interpreted to mean that while the Rat's North sector brings aggravations, you can also expect there to be a good outcome to whatever conflicts do arise.

The Rat sign also enjoys the patronage of the *Tai Sui*, the God of the Year, in its sector. While hosting the Tai Sui can be troublesome due to the "taboos" that need to be observed (keeping the sector quiet and not excessively noisy) the Rat derives many significant benefits from having the support of the Tai Sui.

Note that for the Rat person, it is imperative to carry the **Tai Sui Amulet** at all times, and to display his **plaque**, as well as a pair of **Pi Yao**, chimera-like creatures known to keep the Grand Duke Jupiter happy and assuaged through the year. Place these cures and lucky symbols in the NORTH sector.

Dealing with #7 in the CENTER

The #7 star in the center of the chart must be kept subdued at all costs if you want a peaceful and harmonious household in 2020.

In cosmic astrology, the ancients will refer to this as a year of the "Broken Soldier" which is the way the #7 star number is described.

It brings betrayal, violence and even bloodshed; and anger can easily descend into harmful and violent aggression. The 7 is a Metal Star and is controlled by the element of Water. From a feng shui perspective then, placing **Water** in the center of the house or the living room is highly recommended.

BLUE COLOUR SCHEME FOR THE CENTER:
Note that the recommended colour scheme for the center of the home this year is blue; invest in blue scatter cushions with symbols of protection for the center of the home. You can also place a blue-coloured carpet or throw-rugs in the center of the living area to simulate the presence of the Water element.

We also recommend the following important remedies to keep the 7 well under control:

1. Place the **Blue Elephant & Rhino** with **Talisman Feathers** here. The Elephant and Rhino in blue, the colour of Water, remedies the Loss Star and this year we have designed this pair of guardians with talisman feathers for added protection. The pair also features the **Anti-Robbery Amulet** to keep the home insulated against robbers and intruders.

2. Display the **Kumbum Stupa** in the Center. The #7 star affects everyone this year. It requires the presence of a very strong sacred symbolic cure to ensure families stay protected against its negative influences. The best spiritual remedy for the #7 is the Kumbum Stupa, which subdues all afflictions and ill energies, and invokes the protective presence of many Wisdom and Enlightened Protectors within the home.

This cure is especially important if any family member belongs to an animal sign that suffers from low life force or spirit essence this year.

The Kumbum Stupa transforms your home into a sacred abode so that malevolent influences cannot enter. It attracts multiple blessings that transform negative energies into positive ones, and ensures you do not suffer from unexpected or untoward reversals of fortune.

3. The presence of **King Gesar with the 13 Wermas** is another highly effective presence to have in the home this year. King Gesar is the Warrior Buddha who brings not just protection but prosperity and material success. He is revered in all the lineage texts for his absolute triumph over evil and over one's rivals and enemies, and with his cortege of 13 Wermas (guardian animals), he protects against 13 kinds of danger. Place him in a respectful position in the center of your home, or on your altar.

4. We have also designed the **Blue Mongoose Carpet** to protect wealth and preserve one's family assets in a year dominated by the #7 Loss Star. Because the Loss Star appears in the center sector, its negative effects affect everyone. The Mongoose is the companion of the Wealth Buddhas and brings the symbolism of continued flows of income and expanding prosperity. Place this carpet in the center part of the home, or of any room you spend a lot of time in.

MAKE INCENSE OFFERINGS

Regular incense offerings go a long way to appeasing the local spirits around your home. This is our absolute favorite method of ensuring everything goes smoothly. When you light incense regularly, offering first to the Deities, then to the local spirits around your home, you can depend on their help to assist you in keeping your home and family safe from anyone with ill intentions even entering your home.

You can burn any kind of incense, but incense with white smoke is always best. We have put together a whole collection of incense on our website *www.fsmegamall.com* and in our World of Feng Shui stores for you to choose from. Because incense is such a beneficial remedy to so many things, we have worked hard at expanding our range for all kinds of homes and uses.

Select incense and incense burners that are easy for you to use on a daily basis. Incense also cleanses the air and infuses your living space with powerful and beneficial fragrances.

As you light your incense daily, pronounce the following invocation:

**NAMAH SARVA
TATHAGATHA AVALOKITE
OM SAMBHARA SAMBHARA HUNG**

Beware Quarrelsome Star #3 in the NORTH

This year, the NORTH, the sector of the ruling animal sign of the year the Rat, has the #3 Quarrelsome Star in residence.

The #3 is a Wood Star, and flying into Water element sector, it gets strengthened. Many feng shui masters

The Quarrelsome Star in the North gets strengthened this year and needs to be subdued.

believe that the #3 has the potential to wreak a lot more havoc than even the *Five Yellow* and other misfortune-bringing stars, and in 2020, because its potency gets enhanced, it is more vital than ever that you strongly suppress it. The #3 star brings conflict and misunderstanding, afflicting anyone born in the year of the Rat, as well as anyone whose bedroom, office or study is located in the North. It also affects all homes whose main door is located here, or anyone who spends a lot of time in this sector.

The NORTH part of all homes and living spaces must be kept as quiet as possible this year.

Keep anything that makes sound and noise out of this sector – this means that TVs, stereo systems and musical instruments should not occupy this sector this year; and definitely <u>NO WINDCHIMES here.</u>

CURE FOR THE NORTH
The best cure for the #3 this year is the **Fire Dragon Holding a Fireball**. This Fire Dragon has been designed in resplendent red studded with red jewels and holding Ksiddigarbha's Fireball, making it an effective and quick-acting cure for the negative effects of the #3.

The Dragon is also the astrological ally of the Rat, thus ensuring that any disagreeable energy manifesting in conflict and quarrels get not only suppressed but converted into harmonious interactions instead.

This cure is especially vital for those facing legal problems or lawsuits, or those who are having difficulties dealing with the authorities. Having the Red Dragon with Fireball in the North will ensure the year goes smoothly and harmoniously for you, and insulate you against the ill effects of the #3.

Place the Fire Dragon Holding Fireball in the North to suppress the Quarrelsome Star here.

Place the **Bejewelled Lucky Tortoise** in the North. There is nothing quite like the tortoise to generate unshakeable support luck and protection against harm from anyone who may wish to challenge you.

The tortoise signifies protective support for the home and ensures that residents stay strong and firm, no matter what trials and tribulations come their way.

In lineage texts, the tortoise was also the bearer of the magical Lo Shu square of numbers, which it was said to have carried to Fu Hsi with all the mysteries of feng shui. It is said to conceal within the design motifs on its shell all the secrets of heaven and earth.

Having the presence of the tortoise in the home ensures members of the household do not get harmed by ill flying star changes, protecting family members from illness, aggravations, quarrels and the ill intentions of others.

EAST plays host to the FIVE YELLOW

The other star everyone needs to be careful about is the *wu wang*, the Five Yellow.

SOUTHEAST 6 Heavenly Star	SOUTH 2 THREE KILLINGS Illness	SOUTHWEST SCHOLASTIC LUCK 4 Peach Blossom
EAST WU WANG 5 Five Yellow	CENTER 7 BURGLARY Violence	WEST 9 Completion
NORTHEAST 1 Victory Luck	NORTH TAI SUI 3 Quarrelsome	NORTHWEST 8 Prosperity

The Five Yellow misfortune star occupies the East sector in 2020.

This misfortune star flies to the East this year, affecting all those born under the sign of Rabbit, the eldest son and also, anyone whose homes face the East direction, or whose bedroom, office or study is located here. The East being a Wood sector goes some way to moderating the influence of the Five Yellow, which is an Earth element star, as Wood destroys Earth. But we do not want to "destroy" the wu wang, we want to exhaust its energies, suppressing its hazardous nature while bringing it back to equilibrium.

FIVE YELLOW CURE
This year's **Five Element Pagoda** has been designed with Om Ah Hum, representing the essence of body, speech and mind, filled with more mantras within the pagoda to purify all 3 vital aspects of the environment.

If you have a house that is more than one level, make sure you have a Five Element Pagoda on every floor. Remember to keep the East part of the home free from too much noise, and avoid renovating in this sector this year – no banging, no digging, no knocking, no stereos.

ILLNESS STAR made worse by Fire element of the SOUTH

The Illness Star 2 has flown into the South. This has the effect of strengthening it, as the South is a Fire element sector.

SOUTHEAST	SOUTH	SOUTHWEST
6 Heavenly Star	**2** Illness	SCHOLASTIC LUCK **4** Peach Blossom
EAST WU WANG **5** Five Yellow	CENTER **7** BURGLARY Violence	WEST **9** Completion
NORTHEAST **1** Victory Luck	NORTH TAI SUI **3** Quarrelsome	NORTHWEST **8** Prosperity

The Illness Star of 2020 gets strengthened by the Fire energy of the South.

The #2 being an Earth star gets stronger than ever; and its ill effects, when they afflict you becomes even

89

more dangerous. It is vital to strongly suppress this star number 2 in 2020. All those living in houses facing South, those born in Horse years, and those whose bedrooms or offices are located in this sector need to pay attention to health issues this year. Avoid mosquito-infested areas, do not eat out as often, and avoid gardening during hours when bugs and mosquitoes come out.

The #2 star also brings increased risk of accidents, so those afflicted by this star need to take care when driving, travelling or when taking part in risky sports or activities.

It is recommended to **WEAR AN AMULET** at all times, and to carry the appropriate cures installed in the South of the home and the office. To protect against illness or if you are already sick or feeling unwell, carry the **Wu Lou Garuda Health Amulet**.

If you have elderly members of the family living in the home, it isespecially important to keep this star under control. Move elderly folk out of bedrooms located in the South for the year, and make sure you have ample cures and symbols of health and longevity in the home.

1. Display **Sau, the God of Longevity** with a pair of cranes and holding a Peach and Wu Lou.

Sau is one of the most popular Deities found in many Chinese homes because he symbolizes good health and a smooth and long life. He is one of the three Star Gods comprising Fuk, Luk and Sau, who together represent the triple aspirations of any family – that of wealth, health and happiness. When displayed as a sct, they representa complete life, with the three key aspects needed for ultimate happiness and well-being.

But when the illness star of the year gets strengthened like it does in 2020, it is highly recommended to display Sau with all his symbols of longevity. This includes the Peach, said to contain the nectar of immortality, cranes which represent long life, and the Wu Lou, the gourd of good health that brings an abundance of blessings.

2. Display the **Garuda Bird**, the powerful celestial protector said to subdue illness, disease and spiritual attacks caused by nagas. The Garuda Bird can be displayed on its own, or it can be displayed with Kuan Yin, the Goddess of Mercy.

Anyone who is ill, elderly or frail will benefit from the presence of the Garuda in the home. And anyone who suspects they may be under spiritual attack, or the victim of some kind of black magic, should most definitely have the Garuda Bird in their presence at all times.

Prosperity Originates in the NORTHWEST this year
(bringing wealth luck to the Patriarch)

The wonderfully auspicious good fortune star of 8 has flown into the NORTHWEST, the sector that represents the PATRIARCH.

SOUTHEAST	SOUTH	SOUTHWEST
6	**2** THREE KILLINGS	SCHOLASTIC LUCK **4**
Heavenly Star	*Illness*	*Peach Blossom*
EAST WU WANG	**CENTER**	**WEST**
5	**7** BURGLARY	**9**
Five Yellow	*Violence*	*Completion*
NORTHEAST	**NORTH**	**NORTHWEST**
1	TAI SUI **3**	**8**
Victory Luck	*Quarrelsome*	*Prosperity*

The wealth star blesses the Patriarch or main breadwinner of the family.

This is extremely beneficial for everyone, as good fortune bestowed on the patriarch leads to auspicious luck for the whole family. The NW sector represents the father, the leader and the heads of all households and organizations, and when the number 8 makes its home in this sector, it means the world will be blessed with good and noble leadership.

When this sector is properly activated, it ensures the father figure makes decisions that benefit all who come under him. In the home, the breadwinner will prosper, and in the office, the bosses and managers provide good leadership to their charges. When the #8 is in the NW, it becomes especially important to enhance because the NW is such an important sector, but more than that, the element of METAL of the North weakens the Earth element of the #8.

Earth element enhancers such as **crystal geodes** and **crystal balls** are very lucky placed in the NW this year.

FENG SHUI ENHANCERS FOR THE NW:
1. All houses that face Northwest benefit from the Prosperity Star this year. Activating this sector with **crystals** and **Earth-element enhancers** in 2020 bring double benefit, stimulating the wealth star and at the same time strengthening the luck of the patriarch. If your office or bedroom is located here, it further benefits you with new

prosperity flowing your way. Having a cluster of **6 smooth crystal balls** in the NW will ensure the luck of the patriarch continuously expands, as well as generating fabulously harmonious vibes throughout the home.

2. If you have windows in the NW corner, it is a good idea to hang **faceted crystal balls** in the windows. These will convert the light streaming through the window into rainbow light, which brings incredible blessings for the father and for the whole family.

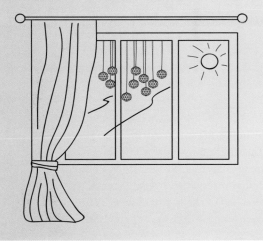

WEALTH ENHANCERS FOR THE NW:

1. The image of a **Golden Rat Holding a Coin** with **"Your Luck Has Arrived"** is an excellent enhancer for the NW, as we are entering the Year of the Golden Rat. Of all the animal signs, the Rat is the most adaptable to change, and in these modern times when technology is moving at such a breakneck pace, the Rat is the best symbol to display if you want to take advantage of new and exciting opportunities opening up. With the Chinese, it is a well-loved tradition to display images of the Rat depicted with coins and ingots, especially in years of the Rat, when this animal is the ruling animal of the year. Remember that the RAT symbolizes having a continuance of wealth!

2. You can also place the **Rat Windchime for Wealth** in the NW. The tinkling sounds of metal on metal activates the wealth star here and also serves to strengthen the energies of the sector. An excellent energiser for this Year of the Rat!

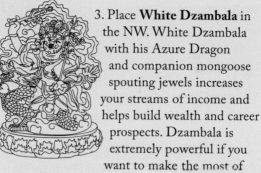

3. Place **White Dzambala** in the NW. White Dzambala with his Azure Dragon and companion mongoose spouting jewels increases your streams of income and helps build wealth and career prospects. Dzambala is extremely powerful if you want to make the most of the Prosperity Star this year. Displaying White Dzambala in the home opens up the cosmic channels for wealth to flow freely into your life! You can also chant his mantra regularly for added potency:

OM PADMA KRODHA AYAH DZAMBALA HRIDAYA HUM PHAT

4. Display the **Rat & Dragon Prosperity "8"** in the NW. The animal sign of the year, the Rat, together with the Chinese Dragon, represents great wealth and prosperity for the coming year. The Rat is the sign that can forage for food and supplies

no matter what the circumstances. The mighty Dragon possesses the courage and confidence to take the big risks that reap the big rewards. Together, Rat and Dragon forming an 8 makes a fabulous wealth enhancer for the home this year.

5. Place the **Lucky Money Frog** on Waterlily Leaf here. The 3-legged money frog sitting on its natural habitat of a waterlily pad symbolizes a continuous flow of income into the household. Place in the NW to activate the wealth energies of the #8, or you can also place anywhere in the home.

6. Invite in **Kuan Kung on Horseback** and display his image in the NW. Kuan Kung is the Warrior Patron Saint of Wealth and his placement in the NW of the home strengthens the luck of the patriarch, which generates excellent feng shui for the whole family. His placement in the NW also activates the #8 Wealth Star here.

WEST represents Future Prosperity & Long-Term Gains
(*for plans with a longer time-frame*)

The West benefits from the presence of the #9 Future Prosperity Star in 2020. This star brings wealth that lasts into the long-term and indicates success for projects and plans with a longer time-frame.

SOUTHEAST	SOUTH	SOUTHWEST
6 Heavenly Star	**2** THREE KILLINGS Illness	SCHOLASTIC LUCK **4** Peach Blossom
EAST	CENTER	WEST
5 WU WANG Five Yellow	**7** BURGLARY Violence	**9** Completion
NORTHEAST	NORTH	NORTHWEST
1 Victory Luck	TAI SUI **3** Quarrelsome	**8** Prosperity

The West brings the luck of long-term gains and asset wealth in 2020.

The #9 is also a magnifying star, so its presence here injects passion and vibrancy to all homes facing West, to those who reside in rooms in the West, and to all born in Rooster years. The number 9 brings new vitality and renewed inspiration, boosting enthusiasm and creativity, and those whose job or purpose requires creativity, new ideas and strong imagination will benefit greatly from the auspicious winds brought by this star.

The only thing one needs to keep in mind is that when an unlucky month star makes an appearance in the WEST this year, the number 9 here can magnify their effects, making bad luck get worse.

In general the West is an extremely lucky sector in 2020; one just needs to be careful in the months of **May, July, September** and **October** when less auspicious stars make an appearance here. In these months, it is best to keep the West less active.

ACTIVATE THE WEST
1. Place the **Wealth Tree with Mongoose & 6 Birds** in the West. This year 2020 has the presence of the Lap Chun which makes this a

good year to get new ideas started and to get new projects off the ground. The placement of a wealth tree ensures that the wealth you attract can grow, so that prosperity is long-lived. We have designed this tree with mongoose spouting jewels with a pile of golden ingots at its base, together with 6 birds to bring new opportunities for wealth creation. The number 6 represents heavenly luck, attracting wealth of a long lasting kind.

When you have wealth luck on your side, it is important to also have opportunities that get that wealth to open up for you. This Wealth Tree enhancer ensures you get every chance to tap that prosperity luck. The mongoose brings the meaning that you can successfully transform all opportunities into riches, that your income streams will be continuous and your wealth can accumulate.

2. If promotion luck is what you want, display the **9 Rank Badges** tabletop enhancer in the West. This symbol brings career success and

allows you to rise to the very top of whatever organization you work at. Those already at managerial level wishing to continue to rise up to a top position should also have the **Monkey sitting on an Elephant** in the West of the office or within sight on the workdesk.

3. Display a pair of **Wealth Cabinets** in the West. Wealth cabinets symbolise having surplus money that you can stow away and grow, ensuring you have not just enough to live on but plenty that you can also use to safeguard your future. This year our wealth cabinets come in red and blue ornamented with golden ingots and coins.

Red brings powerful yang energy and Blue is the colour of Water, the element that is always associated with money luck.

4. Displaying a **Rooster** in the West strengthens the energy of this sector. The Rooster is the epitome of vision, organization and punctuality. The Rooster also has the ability to peck away at productivity-quashing politicking and conflict.

If your office is located in the West, make sure you have a Rooster on your work desk to ensure your path to success and promotion stays free of interference from rivals who may want to take your place.

Those with offices in the West should have a Rooster on their work desk.

NORTHEAST
enjoys Winning Luck
(*to triumph over any competition*)

The Victory Star #1 flies into the Northeast this year, benefitting all homes facing NE, anyone whose bedroom or office is located here, and those born in Ox and Tiger years.

SOUTHEAST	SOUTH	SOUTHWEST
6 THREE KILLINGS *Heavenly Star*	**2** *Illness*	SCHOLASTIC LUCK **4** *Peach Blossom*
EAST	CENTER	WEST
WU WANG **5** *Five Yellow*	**7** BURGLARY *Violence*	**9** *Completion*
NORTHEAST	NORTH	NORTHWEST
1 *Victory Luck*	TAI SUI **3** *Quarrelsome*	**8** *Prosperity*

The NE sector brings "winning" luck in 2020.

The NE is an Earth sector, so the #1 Water Star needs strengthening in the NE, in order to enjoy the full brilliance of its effects. But the presence of the *Winning Star* makes this a very lucky part of any home or premise.

The luck it brings allows one to triumph over any competition, so whenever you find yourself in a situation where you have to compete with others for recognition, business or good will, the energy of this sector helps you along.

1. The best enhancer for this year's #1 Victory Star is the **Windhorse-Boosting Victory Flag**. This flag comes with the King Gesar Mantra with all 5 element colours featured. This enhancer ensures you not only survive the competition but triumph over it in outstanding manner. Vital for anyone who has rivals of any kind.

Windhorse-Boosting
Victory Flag

2. Place the **Luo Han with Crab** in the NE. The Luo Han with Crab is one of the well-known 18 Chinese Saints who bring good fortune in their distinctive forms. The Luo Han with Crab helps by bringing you excellent strategic thinking. It helps all entrepreneurs and executives make all the right decisions.

Having the Luo Han with Crab in the home imbues one with formidable intellect and great strategy and allows whoever taps on his power to rise up to high positions of rank and influence. All those with ambitions in the corporate field should have this Luo Han nearby. Place in the NE this year.

3. **Liu Bei**, the founder of the Shu-Han Dynasty during the Three Kingdom Periods is another extremely effective and auspicious symbol for the NE. Liu Bei was famous for bringing peace and prosperity to China during the Han Dynasty and well-known for his superior intellect and strategic acumen. Fantastic enhancer for the NE in 2020.

SOUTHEAST
is blessed by the Heavens
(as well as Big Auspicious)

The Heavenly Star #6 flies into the Southeast, the sector of the Dragon and Snake. These two animal signs benefit from this star's benevolent influence, which means more opportunities coming their way, and more people working behind the scenes helping them.

The Southeast enjoys blessings from heaven.
Activate with Jade Emperor Heaven Amulet.

107

The Heaven Star also brings superior mentor and benefactor luck, so whatever the path you set out on, you will find bounteous help and assistance along the way.

When you enjoy the benefits of the #6 star, even if a path does not seem well-defined, you can have the confidence to venture forth, because things will have their own way of falling into place. All those living in homes facing SE, or whose bedroom or office is located in the SE will benefit from this star directly. Every home should make every endeavour to keep this part of the house active and filled with life. Do not "lock up" this auspicious star in some store room!

The SE is also the place of the eldest daughter of the family, who benefits from the cosmic luck of the heavens this year.

ACTIVATE THE HEAVEN STAR
1. Place the **Wealth Bull** in the SE. The Wealth Bull is the sacred buffalo of the Buddhas who bestows heightened spiritual perception and understanding, allowing you to spot the big opportunities when they come your way. It gives you the wisdom and the self-assuredness you will need to make the best decisions in all situations.

When you have the Wealth Bull on your side, it makes you invincible to enemies and strong in the face of competition. It gives you the will and the savvy to make the most of all your openings, allowing you to turn Big Auspicious into big breaks. It infuses you with the energies of big success, makes you feel more alive and is the best enhancer for anyone with low levels of life force or spirit essence.

Its **deep blue colour** represents the Water element, which syncs nicely with the Wood element chi of the SE.

Place the Wealth Bull in the SE in 2020.

2. For business success, display the **Double Humped Camel**. This symbol is a must-have for anyone in business as it ensures you always maintain a healthy cash flow.

To be able to benefit from the opportunities that come your way, you must be financially secure and have a large enough war chest to ensure you can weather any turbulence ortemporary downturn in luck. Having the Double Humped Camel in your vicinity brings the qualities of steadfastness and financial security. It will ensure you can take the risks you need to take to make it really big!

3. All those whose bedrooms are located in the SE should carry or wear the **Lock Coin Amulet.** While there are big opportunities coming, the appearance of the *Robbery Star* from the 24 Mountains warns of danger of loss. Ensure all your risks are calculated and do not bite off more than you can chew. One step at a time is the way forward; then build on each step. Don't try to get ahead of yourself.

4. Display the **Jade Emperor with Qui Ren Talisman** for everything to go smoothly for you. Place in the SE sector of the home to capture all of heaven's auspicious blessings.

111

Peach Blossom Luck in the SOUTHWEST
(brings marriage opportunities)

Love and romance is in the air in the Southwest this year! The Peach Blossom Star #4 makes an appearance here and because this is also the Universal Love Corner as following the original Lo Shu pattern of the Yang Pa Kua, this makes its potency all the more effective!

SOUTHEAST	SOUTH	SOUTHWEST
6	**2** THREE KILLINGS	**4**
Heavenly Star	Illness	Peach Blossom
EAST	CENTER	WEST
5 WU WANG	**7** BURGLARY	**9**
Five Yellow	Violence	Completion
NORTHEAST	NORTH	NORTHWEST
1	TAI SUI **3**	**8**
Victory Luck	Quarrelsome	Prosperity

The Peach Blossom Star flies into the SW, bringing marriage opportunities.

Anyone living in the SW of homes has the potential to find love and to get married, if that is what you want!

The Peach Blossom Star makes you more sociable and more attuned to romance and romantic inclinations. It will make anyone residing in this sector more amenable to love and to matters of the heart.

The Southwest is also the sector of the Sheep and Monkey, so this year, these two animal signs benefit from enhanced opportunities for marriage and settling down. Those of marriageable age and looking for a partner should step up their efforts this year.

ENHANCING FOR LOVE IN THE SW:

1. If you are looking for a partner, place the **Red Tara Home Amulet** in the SW of your home.  Filled with her precious mantras and then sealed, having her in the home invokes her sacred qualities and her presence. One of the manifestations of Red Tara is *Kurukulle*, the ultimate female Buddha with the power to

help all those in search of love and a soulmate. She improves your relationships with friends, colleagues, bosses and anyone else you deal with, and attracts true love into your life.

2. You can also display the **Banner of Love** featuring **Kurukulle,** the beautiful Goddess of Love. When shown holding her bow and arrow made of flowers, she is powerful indeed. Invoking her help boosts one's magnetism and charisma. If you have her image in the home and regularly call on her help, you will start to find everyone becoming friendlier towards you, bonding with you better, and your words and opinions will start counting for more in all discussions and discourses you have.

3. For those who wish to attract marriage opportunities

into your life, or who wish to rekindle a tired marriage, display the **Double Happiness Symbol** or carry in your pocket.

4. For those already married, there is no better symbol than **Marriage Happiness Ducks**. These colourful ducks bring not just marital happiness; they light up your life and help you see all the beauty and good qualities in each other. They also subdue disharmony energies that cause quarrels and arguments. Essential symbol for the home of any married couple, as it ensures you stay happily married. It strengthens your love for one another and brings plenty of joy and good times to the marriage.

5. If you are looking for love and have your eye on someone, carry the **9-Tailed White Fox Amulet** to make you irresistible. This amulet will smooth you irresistible. This amulet will smooth your path to happiness in love.

SOUTHWEST
also brings scholastic success
(for students & those taking exams)

The #4 star also brings scholastic and academic Success. Those who benefit from the Peach Blossom aspects of this star will likewise benefit from the potential for scholastic achievements it bestows. Young Sheep and Monkey children in school benefit from study luck this year.

SOUTHEAST	SOUTH	SOUTHWEST
6	**2** THREE KILLINGS	SCHOLASTIC LUCK **4**
Heavenly Star	*Illness*	*Peach Blossom*
EAST	CENTER	WEST
5 WU WANG	**7** BURGLARY	**9**
Five Yellow	*Violence*	*Completion*
NORTHEAST	NORTH	NORTHWEST
1	TAI SUI **3**	**8**
Victory Luck	*Quarrelsome*	*Prosperity*

The SW is excellent for students this year.
Brings exam success and scholastic accolades.

The #4 also brings greater creativity to those in lines of work that involve research, knowledge accumulation and application of that knowledge. The creativity imbues you with greater ability to think outside the box, so you do not just learn up knowledge but add to it.

1. Place the **Scholar on Dragon Carp** in the SW. Shown with the *four symbols of scholarship*, this activator brings exam success and top academic attainment to those pursuing exams. To the Chinese, the Dragon Carp is the ultimate symbol of achievement and the 4 Scholastic Objects – the book, scroll, brush and flute – represent a balanced and well-rounded education.

Scholar on
Dragon Carp

All homes with children of school or college-going age should have this symbol placed in the SW of the house or of their study room this year.

2. For children finding it difficult to get or stay motivated in studies, we recommend the **Red Wisdom Pagoda.** This pagoda generates enthusiasm and self-discipline, ensuring teenagers and young adults do not get side-tracked into unproductive activities, and do not fall under the influence of unsuitable company. Place in the SW of the home or study room of your teenager.

3. If you wish to call on spiritual help, you should invite in **Manjushri, the Buddha of Wisdom and Knowledge** into your home. He cuts through ignorance and brings understanding to all who seek it. Students pursuing top exam grades can call on his help to invoke his blessings. Place on an altar in the home or

in a respectable place in the SW in 2020. You can also wear the **Wealth and Wisdom Mantra Ring** which features Manjushri's mantra on the inside and Dzambala's mantra on the outside.

Learn up Manjushri's mantra and chant 108 times each day. Best to get a dedicated mala if you can. Whenever trying to access knowledge that's at the edge of your consciousness, e.g. in an exam situation, chant his mantra and let him bring the answer to you.

OM AH RA PA CHA NA DHI

Afflictions to watch out for...
TAI SUI in the North

The Tai Sui or Grand Duke Jupiter, also known as the God of the Year, assists the Jade Emperor in helping and controlling the mortal world. The Tai Sui is usually regarded as the *Heavenly General*, although his personality, disposition and position within the compass changes from year to year.

The Tai Sui resides in the North in 2020.

In 2020, TAI SUI resides in the NORTH, the place of the Rat. This bestows on all those born under the sign of RAT his heavenly blessings and protection.

However, the animal sign directly opposite the Rat, i.e. the HORSE, usually risks thefull wrath of the Tai Sui as this is deemed to be confronting this powerful Year God. Many Taoists also believe that it is not just the animal sign directly facing the Tai Sui of the year that risks offending the Tai Sui. All four animals that form a cross with the conflicting animal sign are at risk.

In 2020 therefore, the cardinal animals of **Horse, Rabbit, Rooster** and **Rat** all need to be mindful that they take steps to appease the Tai Sui. Especially the HORSE, who directly confronts the Tai Sui!

To get Tai Sui onto your side, we always recommend having a pair of **heavenly Pi Yao** in his

location – in 2020, place a pair of Pi Yao in the North. You should also place the **image of the year's Tai Sui** here.

We have made his image into a plaque to display in the home, and also as a portable amulet to carry throughout the day. Note that the Tai Sui changes each year, and in all, there are sixty Tai Sui. It is important to pay attention to this important dimension of your feng shui update each year.

THREE KILLINGS in the South

The Three Killings can be a troublesome affliction when you ignore it, because it brings 3 kinds of losses – loss of wealth, loss of your good name and reputation, and loss of someone you love.

The 3 Killings cause troubles to come not in ones and twos but, as Shakespeare said, in "battalions" -

The Three Killings resides in the South in 2020, bringing 3 kinds of bad luck. It MUST be suppressed.

resembling a 3-pronged attack at three important dimensions of happiness.

In 2020, this affliction enters the SOUTH, anyone whose house faces South, or whose bedroom or office is located South will be affected by its negative energies. This is an important affliction to control, because its effects can be devastatingly severe. It is important to keep it under control.

This year we recommend the **Three Celestial Bells** featuring the three guardians – the Pi Yao, Chi Lin and Fu Dog. Bells of this size and shape are powerful cures; they also signify achievement in the face of great obstacles.

Place the 3 Celestial Bells in the South sector this year to suppress the Three Killings.

The symbolism of the bells is truly powerful as the sound of these bells completely annihilates all bad vibrations, especially those caused by the 3 Killings affliction. These bells also protect you from bad intentions aimed your way by those jealous of your success or situation.

Do NOT have your back to the SOUTH this year. This means you MUST NOT face North even if it is a "good" direction for you according to your Kua. Doing so could cause you to get "hit" by the Three Killings!

CHAPTER

5

RAT INTERACTING WITH OTHERS IN 2020

RAT'S RELATIONSHIPS WITH OTHER SIGNS IN 2020
Getting along despite your argumentative nature

To the Chinese, especially when searching for a marriage partner, few things matter more to a bride or groom's parents than compatibility of horoscopes between their child and the potential partner. Indeed, when match-making, the first thing one would look at are the animal signs of the potential couple and further to that, the Paht Chee charts of the couple.

When you look at not just the year of birth but all four pillars of birth, superficial incompatibilities can be overcome, just like seeming dream pairings may not be all that first meets the eye. Understanding how all this works helps one ensure that any partnership you enter into stands the best chance of harmony, success and longevity.

In today's world, it is not just marriage where astrological compatibilities are investigated. One can use these methods to ensure a new employee can get along with the team, to examine pros and cons before entering a joint venture, or even which friends you can trust more than others.

For couples having children, planning the best years to conceive can boost chances of siblings getting along nicely, children staying filial to their parents and bringing honour, pride and happiness to the family.

SHORT VS LONG RUN COMPATIBILITY

While major compatibilities (and mismatches) tend to hold true in the longer run, the nuances of relationships nevertheless ebb and flow and change from year to year. When one is going through a good year, it makes it easier to get along with others in general. Natural affinity gets enhanced and incompatibilities are reduced when stars align in your favour.

In the short term, while two animal signs may not jive well following the traditional understanding of horoscopes, their luck patterns may merge nicely for a particular year, which enables them to achieve success when they team up. This kind of fluctuating compatibility is useful when checking whether or not to join forces for a short-term project, or to team up for a set transitory period. Understanding how relationship affinities fluctuate will also help you avoid getting stuck with someone who is evidently unsuited to you, but who you may fall head over heels over in the short term. When warned not to let things get too serious, you may want to hold out and test a particular relationship a little longer before committing to say marriage or a formal business partnership.

Being aware of the tones and gradations of astrological compatibilities will also allow you to understand people's reactions better, which will let you improve relations with those already in your life whether you like it or not.

Gaining a solid understanding of feng shui astrology gives you practical methods to nullify any relationship afflictions you may face.

For instance, if you are already married with children but struggling to keep the peace in the marriage, there are remedies that can make your already existing union more harmonious.

We discuss all the major compatibilities to take note of, and then we look at the RAT and its compatibility with each of the 12 different animal signs in 2020.

COMPATIBILITY GROUPINGS

1. TRIANGLES OF AFFINITY - *great support*

2. ASTROLOGICAL SOULMATES - *power friendship*

3. SECRET FRIENDS - *influencing each other*

4. SEASONAL TRINITIES - *wealth-enhancing*

5. PEACH BLOSSOM LINKS - *romance*

6. YOUR ZODIAC ENEMY - *astrological foes*

1. TRIANGLES OF ALLIES

There are four triangles of affinity made up of three animals signs. Each grouping possesses similar traits, reactions and belief systems that create natural bonds between them. Their thought processes are similar, and their aims and life goals coincide. When you belong to the same triangle of affinity, you are bound to get long well and be naturally supportive of one another.

Animal signs that belong to the same affinity triangle are set four years apart, and when planning to have children, a good way to ensure they all get along is to plan a four-year age gap between them.

The four sets of affinity triangles are as follows:

COMPETITORS Rat, Dragon, Monkey	Ambitious, Brilliant, Tough
THINKERS Ox, Snake, Rooster	Generous, Focused, Resilient
ADVENTURERS Dog, Tiger, Horse	Ethical, Brave, Loyal
DIPLOMATS Boar, Sheep, Rabbit	Creative, Kind, Emotional

AFFINITY TRIANGLE OF COMPETITORS

The RAT belongs to the affinity triangle of COMPETITORS, together with the DRAGON and MONKEY. These are the action-oriented group of the Zodiac who can always be counted upon to get things done. You are full of initiative with inherent self-confidence. Your determination rivals anyone's, and when you find yourself in a competitive situation, you always rise to the occasion. You never give up without a fight and use your natural charisma and charm to help you along. While you are deadly serious in any rivalry, you always manage to win the race with a good sense of humour. It is difficult to abhor you when you come out tops, because you are so innately likeable.

When someone of the Rat sign gets together with a Dragon or Monkey, while your competitive traits get enhanced, it will not be against each other. It will be a case of you and your allies against the world.

When you team up with anyone from your triangle of affinity, there will be literally no stopping you! Any pairing of Rat with either Dragon or Monkey will last and last; while you may have your temporary temper tantrums that could send one or both of you flying off the handle, you will be back in each other's arms in no time at all..

2. ASTROLOGICAL SOULMATES

There are six pairs of astrological soulmates in the Chinese Zodiac, with each pairing creating a special talent when they come together. It is easy to find happiness in the arms of your soulmate. In each pair, a yin generates perfect balance with its yang counterpart. Each pair is known as a Zodiac House, and within each pair a very special cosmic bond is created when they come together. Any marriage, business partnership or friendship between two signs from the same house results in a relationship whose sum is far greater than its individual parts.

The RAT and OX form the *House of Creativity & Cleverness*. Together these two are an unstoppable pair. There is plenty of stratagem and action, so whatever ideas are hatched are quickly put to good use. The Rat gets things started and the Ox always works to complete what is started. They make a formidable pair indeed as husband and wife, but even more than that, as a united front against anyone who may stand up against them.

ANIMALS	YIN/ YANG	ZODIAC HOUSE CREATED	TALENTS UNLEASHED
RAT & OX	YANG/ YIN	**House of Creativity and Cleverness**	The Rat initiates The Ox completes
TIGER & RABBIT	YANG/ YIN	**House of Growth and Development**	The Tiger uses strength The Rabbit uses negotiation
DRAGON & SNAKE	YANG/ YIN	**House of Magic and Spirituality**	The Dragon takes action The Snake creates magic
HORSE & SHEEP	YANG/ YIN	**House of Passion and Sexuality**	The Horse embodies strength & courage The Sheep embodies seduction & allure
MONKEY & ROOSTER	YANG/ YIN	**House of Career and Commerce**	The Monkey creates good strategy The Rooster takes timely action
DOG & BOAR	YANG/ YIN	**House of Domesticity**	The Dog creates alliances The Boar benefits

Rat and Ox can work together professionally as colleagues and associates. As siblings or friends, they are equals in every way, and should they embark on something together, they easily meet with great success. As lovers, they constantly find new ways of stimulating one another. Rat's ingenuity joins up well with Ox's endurance, and they can last the long haul together, never losing whatever initial spark brought them together in the first place.

3. SECRET FRIENDS

There are six pairs of secret friends in the Chinese Zodiac and they are extraordinarily compatible. When they become lovers or friends, they genuinely have each other's best interests at heart. There is no malice, no rivalry and no distrust at all.

Secret friends need no acknowledgement when they help each other out, hence the RAT will always be friends with the OX.

Rat and Ox are secret friends of the Zodiac.

SECRET FRIENDS

RAT & OX

RABBIT & DOG

HORSE & SHEEP

TIGER & BOAR

DRAGON & ROOSTER

SNAKE & MONKEY

For the RAT, your secret friend the OX is someone who will help you out without your even knowing. When taking advice from your secret friend, you can be sure they have no ulterior motive when offering their opinion. There is a lot of trust between secret friends, and for the Rat and the Ox, your bond is even more powerful, as you are also Astrological Soulmates. The Rat benefits from Ox's steadfastness, while the Ox benefits from Rat's quick thinking. Each sign should display their secret friend in the home to boost the power of this pairing.

4. SEASONAL GROUPINGS

There are four seasonal trinity combinations of signs that bring exceptional luck during certain seasons. Such luck usually manifests as wealth luck. Many experts consider these to be one of the more powerful combination of animal signs, but their effects are multiplied when all three are present. Hence this astrological affinity works better in groups of three than between couples.

When two parents and a child, for instance, each belong to a different animal belonging to the same Seasonal group, this will tend to manifest as wealth luck for the family. This also works when a trio get together for a business or commercial venture – their affinity manifests as mutual success for all three.

It is necessary for all three to live together or work in the same office in close proximity for the pattern of prosperity to take effect. For greater impact, it is better if all are using the direction associated with the relevant seasons. Thus the seasonal combination of Spring is East, while the seasonal combination of Summer is South.

The table below summarises the seasonal groupings.

ANIMALS	SEASON	ELEMENT/DIRECTION
Tiger, Rabbit, Dragon	Spring	Wood/East
Snake, Horse, Sheep	Summer	Fire/South
Monkey, Rooster, Dog	Autumn	Metal/West
Rat, Ox, Boar	Winter	Water/North

The RAT belongs to the seasonal combination of WINTER, a combination which further strengthens its links with the OX, with whom the Rat is both a secret friend and a soulmate, and the BOAR. When Rat and Ox marry and they have a Boar child for instance, the three together form the Trinity of Winter. This means they are not only exceptionally close but attract the luck of wealth and abundance during the winter season.

5. PEACH BLOSSOM LINKS

Each of the alliances of allies has a special relationship with one of the four cardinal signs of Horse, Rat, Rooster and Rabbit. These are the symbolic representations of love and romance for one alliance group of animal signs. In the horoscope, they are referred to as Peach Blossom Animals and the presence of their image in the home of the matching alliance of allies brings Peach Blossom Luck, which symbolizes love and romance.

The RAT belongs to the alliance of Dragon, Monkey and Rat, and for them, the ROOSTER is their Peach Blossom Animal.

The Rat benefits from associating with anyone born in a Rooster year and will also gain from placing an **image of a Rooster** in the West part of the house. Displaying a **Peach Blossom Rooster** in the West attracts marriage luck to the Rat-born.

Meanwhile, the Rat is itself also a primary animal sign, and is itself the Peach Blossom Animal of the alliance of Rabbit, Boar and Sheep. Hence, it also has a Peach Blossom connection to these animal signs.

6. YOUR ZODIAC ENEMY

There is a six year gap between natural enemies. A marriage between them is not usually recommended. When you get together with your zodiac enemy, it will be difficult for you to make your union last because there are so many inherent infidelities. Zodiac enemies, even if you start out as the best of friends or the most infatuated of lovers, will tend to fall out or grow apart over time. You are not inherently suited to one another, so the advice is not to start anything serious in the first place.

Do not leave yourself vulnerable to your zodiac enemy, because they can hurt you without even meaning to. Indeed, arguments and fall-outs between zodiac foes have far longer-lasting effects than any other pairs of animal signs. Differences are magnified, and conflicts are uglier.

The RAT's Zodiac Enemy is the HORSE, so it is best for Rat to not get too close to a Horse. In a marriage, this union is unlikely to bring lasting happiness unless other indications in their Paht Chee or other charts suggest otherwise. In a business partnership, this pairing is likely to lead to problems, sometimes ending in lengthy litigation and plenty of bad blood.

ZODIAC ENEMIES

RAT & HORSE

RABBIT & ROOSTER

OX & SHEEP

TIGER & MONKEY

DRAGON & DOG

SNAKE & BOAR

This year in 2020, Rat and Horse are particularly hostile towards one another. BEWARE!

ENEMY REMEDY: If you are already in some kind of relationship with your zodiac enemy, the best remedy is to display the secret friend of your astrological enemy. For the RAT in a relationship with a HORSE, you should display the secret friend of the Horse, i.e. the SHEEP near you.

CHAPTER FIVE

ANNUAL INFLUENCES
to the Horoscope Compatibilities

Annual energies affect what kind of people you have greater or lesser affinity with. In some years, you could feel an inexplicable aversion to someone you have always liked; or a sudden attraction to someone you have always found infuriating! Usually, affinity groupings, secret friend alliances and soulmate pairings exert strong influences, but annual energy changes also have the power to influence your thinking and the way you behave or react to others. These changes can make you more argumentative or more affectionate, more impatient or more considerate.

Personal luck also influences how we act around others. When life and work goes well, we become better disposed to those in our orbit. When luck is riding high, even a Zodiac enemy can become a good friend, even if only for a short period. Likewise, when one is being challenged by major problems or obstacles, even the slightest provocation can lead to anger. Even Zodiac friends and allies might then appear to be insufferable. A falling-out between horoscope allies is thus not impossible when the energies go against you.

In the following section, we examine Rat's personal relationships with other signs in 2020.

RAT'S RELATIONSHIPS WITH OTHER SIGNS IN 2020

PAIRINGS	COMPATIBILITY IN 2020
RAT & RAT	Quarrelsome but auspicious
RAT & OX	Rat benefits from Ox's restful nature
RAT & TIGER	Tiger lends strength to the Rat
RAT & RABBIT	A difficult pair. Not ideal!
RAT & DRAGON	Allies always great together!
RAT & SNAKE	Long-lasting bond in a year full of surprises
RAT & HORSE	Astrological foes meet noisy year!
RAT & SHEEP	Sheep in control of this relationship
RAT & MONKEY	Best of pals on a roll!
RAT & ROOSTER	Much bliss and happiness to be had
RAT & DOG	Ho Tu brings this pair good fortune
RAT & BOAR	Happy year for these two Water signs

RAT/RAT *suppress anger energies*

Quarrelsome but auspicious time for two Rats

Rats can get along with others of its own sign, but this amiable trait will not be so apparent in its own Year of the Rat 2020. The energies brought by the constellations indicate stresses and strains to the relationship, and plenty of arguments galore. While it will be an irritable year for two Rats, success is possible and even probable. But the path to getting there will a meandering one fraught with aggravation and struggle.

> In 2020, Rat has the troublesome #3 Quarrelsome Star in its sector, and when two Rats get together, it can be double the trouble.

The energies of the year are not in sync with two Rats working together amicably, and should you be thrown together in a work situation, it would be best for you to divide up the work and come together only for brief update meetings. Working in regular discussion mode will only drive the both of you round the bend. But the ironic thing is that two Rats working together in 2020 is a recipe for great success! You enjoy special affinity with the year ruled by the #7, and two Rats together will deliver double the goods - if you don't tear each other's throats out in the meantime! Make sure you work at keeping your temper in check or you risk ruining what could be a really good thing.

Two Rats in a love relationship face the same trials and tribulations as those in any other kind of relationship this year. Your temper is bad; and egged on by another sorry tempered soul will only make things worse. The Rat couple already together could face difficult times ahead, but in the longer term, two Rats do get along well, with many shared interests and common traits. If already together, it is worth weathering the temporary storm to enjoy sunnier times ahead.

Two **48 year old Water Rats** have the biggest chance of a harmonious year together. Your combined Water element energy tempers your egos and suppresses the difficult dominant 7 star. Two **36 year old Wood Rats** can also get along, but will need to work harder to keep tempers in check. The **27 year old Fire Rat** is likely more focused on career ambitions, and it is probably better this way.

> **LOVE ENHANCER:** Wear plenty of **Red** to quell the argumentative energies that plague you this year. For two Rats in love, get a pair of **Marriage Happiness Ducks** to smooth things along.

RAT/OX *secret friends & soulmates*
Rat benefits from Ox's restful nature

The Rat and Ox enjoy one of the more special relationships in the Zodiac. You two are soulmates as well as secret friends, so whatever year the two of you happen to be going through will not change the kind of relationship you two enjoy. Yours will always be a supportive pairing, and if a Rat finds an Ox to share a lifetime with, the advice is to never let this one go.

Together, Rat and Ox have the kind of relationship other couples only dream of. Unquestioning loyalty and compatible personality traits make this a union that lasts well into the long term.

Astrologically, these two signs have multiple robust connections with one another, and in 2020, all these affinities get enhanced. Of the two, it will be the Ox that is feeling stronger, which much better element luck indications than its astrological soulmate the Rat, but it has plenty of strength enough for the two of them. Ox enjoys more than just strong life force and spirit essence, it also has the Victory Star on its side. The Rat together with someone of the Ox sign will find itself calmer, and much less likely to explode in anger or frustration.

Ox plays confidante to the Rat, and this pairing works just as well in a work, friend or sibling situation as it does in a love relationship. When Rat and Ox get together, their nature is to build. When faced with any difficulty, instead of arguing who is right, their ideas combine to produce the best solution to whatever predicament they may be facing. They make an excellent team, and when pitted against the outside world, nobody stands a chance between these two.

2020 sees the Ox blessed with much good fortune, which it is only too happy to share with its Rat partner. Both bring something unique to the pairing, with Ox bringing stability and Rat bringing effervescence. These two find happiness in each other's arms no matter what the weather.

The **48 year old Water Rat** with the **47 year old Water Ox** make an especially prolific pairing in 2020, with both enjoying excellent wealth luck and very good other indications - these two working together have the opportunity to reach highly elevated status in society, politics or the circles they move in. The **36 year old Wood Rat** with the **25 year old Wood Ox** enjoy personal happiness together but combine better in love than in work. But any pairing between any Rat and Ox will not go far wrong.

RAT/TIGER *good balance*
Tiger lends strength to Rat in 2020

While at first glance there may not appear all that much in common between Rat and Tiger, theirs is a pairing that simply works. It is a case of opposites attracting, and in 2020 this attraction only grows. The Tiger, the more rambunctious of the two, admires the steady dependability of the Rat. The Rat meanwhile is mesmerised by the ardent charisma of the Tiger.

Rat & Tiger form one of those relationships that may not appear likely at first glance. Yet once you're together you become really quite inseparable, and the energies of 2020 only fuel this mutual attraction between you two.

In 2020, it will be Tiger who takes the lead, and Rat will gladly follow. For the Rat, the Tiger is a nice distraction from everything that may appear wrong with life, and while outwardly the Tiger is all showy bravado, in private with a Rat partner, there is a highly sentimental side to this big cat.

Tiger is able to play loud or soft when with a Rat, singing to many different tunes. Rat uncovers the many different layers of Tiger's personality, unveiling all that is positive under any cattish demeanour.

★★★★

In 2020, Tiger enjoys a winning streak which gets boosted by Rat's unfailing admiration, while Rat's quarrelsome demeanour gets quelled by Tiger's high spirited positivity.

The coming year sees Tiger gain strength, emerging from a successful past year stronger than ever, and with a Rat companion, Tiger is able to focus on yet more upward momentum. With a Rat partner, the Tiger feels less need to show off, and this is when its real talents can get unleashed. Rat's intrinsic Water energy fuels Tiger's vitality, while Tiger's success inspires and motivates the Rat.

This year you do not have the external Peach Blossom causing problems like last year, and while Rat may be more hot-tempered than usual, its anger will be unlikely to be directed at a Tiger mate. Love gets every opportunity to grow.

In 2020, Rat and Tiger can climb mountains together and even make a go at something more long term. Marriage is definitely a possibility, but for things to get taken to the next level, it will be up to the Tiger to make the first move. This is a relationship that works well whether in love or at work, and the more Rat lets Tiger take the lead, the happier will be the pairing. Enjoy the year for there are only good things in store!

RAT/RABBIT *stressful*

A noisy pairing in 2020! Not ideal.

Rat and Rabbit face a tough year ahead, and when put together, it only adds more fuel to the fire. Rat has the *#3 Quarrelsome Star* to contend with, while Rabbit suffers the trials and tribulations brought by the troublesome *Five Yellow*. Because neither are having an easy time, neither will have to time to play support group or shoulder to cry on to the other.

> Both Rat and Rabbit have a hot streak, and when they come together in 2020, conflict energies simply get heightened. While they may enjoy other years together, this is not one where getting cosy brings benefits to either.

These two cardinal signs have the most difficult flying stars in their respective sectors, and hell hath no fury when their tempers get set off. Theirs is a noisy relationship that riles up not just each other but everyone in their circle. The advice is to stay well out of each other's way in this coming year. If you are already together, work at suppressing your irritability. Even if there are initial sparks of attraction, things get heated rather quickly with these two this year, and a friendship or relationship that could've gone somewhere could get irreparably damaged should you attempt to pursue something deeper with each other. The Wood energies of the Rabbit fuel the quarrelsome star afflicting the Rat, and when Rat gets angry, Rabbit will not be in any kind of forgiving mood. The Rabbit always gives as good as it gets, so Rat best stay far away from its woodland friend this year.

The constellations are simply not on their side most of the time, and as a result, both Rat and Rabbit find their time together stressful and onerous. Rat is already feeling fragile with low levels of element luck, and a Rabbit partner does nothing to improve matters.

Rabbit on the other hand enjoys superlative levels of life force and spirit essence but will not be in the mood to share its successes with a Rat mate. It's *wu wang* affliction suppresses its generosity this way, and Rabbit is more likely to taunt Rat with its successes than use them to help Rat.

If the two happen to be in a relationship, **Anti-Anger Amulets** are badly needed. Rabbit will not feel the negative effects of this destructive pairing so acutely as Rat but will find most other signs easier to get along with this year. Rat meanwhile should steer clear.

RAT/DRAGON *powerful together*
Allies always supporting one another

Rat and Dragon always support one another, and this year is no different. Beyond being astrological allies and each other's greatest supporters, there's a whole lot more in store for this pair of natural friends. Whether they come together as a romantic couple, business partners, parent and child, or siblings, they will always be close, and will stand by each other through good times and bad.

Rat and Dragon possess a very special rapport, which gets enhanced by the auspicious winds blowing in Dragon's direction in 2020. This is a year when these two can easily take their relationship to the next level should they wish to.

While this is usually a relationship of equals, this year it pays to let Dragon take the lead. Dragon is the stronger of the two in terms of flying star indications as well as element luck. From the 24 mountains, the Dragon enjoys the blessings of the *Big Auspicious*, indicating success of a windfall nature. Good tidings come unexpectedly, and Rat provides a grounding influence amidst some head-turning opportunities and revelations. This year, Dragon may be the more high

profile of the two, but Rat will always provide valuable support from the sidelines. Roles may get reversed in another year, but this is what's so beautiful about this pair; both are totally selfless when with each other, and the success of one will never breed jealousy in the other. Rat and Dragon are true friends whose natural affinity always kicks in to save the day.

In a year that proves trickier for Rat than Dragon, it will be Dragon who constantly boosts Rat's mood and confidence. But while Dragon plays frontman this year, it does not forget or belittle what Rat does for it behind the scenes.

When working together, they make a formidable team, and even in a year when Rat may suffers much weaker vitality than Dragon, it pulls its weight in this partnership. These two have the uncanny ability to divide up their roles so neither ends up competing with the other, despite both being "competitors" by nature.

When Rat and Dragon share goals and ambitions, you can be sure they will achieve them; the only question being how quickly. Riding on Dragon's good fortune, if Rat correctly recognises it has to take a backseat, it will likely prove sooner rather than later.

RAT/SNAKE *Mysterious connection*

Long-lasting bond in a year full of surprises

While there are no overtly obvious common traits or even common interests between these two, Rat and Snake always enjoy a mysterious connection that survives despite the odds. Theirs is a pairing of opposites - Rat's Water and Snake's Fire are elementally incompatible, but instead of Water putting out the Fire, when Rat and Snake get together, the Fire turns the Water into steam.

Nothing is as it first seems when a Rat gets together with a Snake. Theirs will be a quirky relationship, one that continues to surprise mutual friends and onlookers, but the bond they share is long-lasting despite their lack of decipherable common denominator.

Snake is a natural charmer and the Rat lets itself get charmed. In 2020 when Rat is plagued by the quarrelsome #3 star, it finds respite in the non-judgemental Snake. There is great warmth in this relationship and this has nothing to do with any special affinity between the two. Their compatibility does not follow any relationship norms, and third parties who wish to snag Rat or Snake from the arms of the other will find it tough indeed.

★★★★

In 2020, while neither enjoy particularly exciting element luck levels, Snake has better other indications than Rat. Snake enjoys a Big Auspicious from the 24 Mountains, as well as the blessings of the Heavenly Star in its sector. Things come more easily to the Snake than the Rat, who has to sing for its supper so to speak.

But while neither Rat nor Snake have a smooth ride in 2020, together they weather the storms better and come out successful in whatever they choose to pursue. Rat has completion luck on its side, while Snake faces its truly big break if its luck can hold.

Because these two are a naturally high-achieving pair, they will not be content just playing house with one another. Their relationship while caring and loveable gets taken to a whole other level if they can pursue and achieve some goal together.

Their inner ambitious natures make the Rat and Snake even better partners in work and business than as lovers. In 2020 when Rat and Snake work together in some commercial venture, Snake becomes a calming influence on the clever but frustrated Rat, while Rat's meticulous and well-disciplined personality gets Snake moving and on track.

RAT/HORSE *Arguments galore*
Astrological foes meet with noisy year!

The Rat and Horse are Zodiac enemies and while last year these two may have developed an uncharacteristic connection, this year all that affinity flies out the window. Rat and Horse are positioned in the Zodiac wheel diametrically opposite one another, and this seems to seal its fate when it comes to getting along this year or in the longer term.

As long as Rat and Horse keep each other at arm's length, they can eat, drink, laugh and enjoy a socially pleasant time together. But when these two attempt to get any closer, cracks appear and the trouble begins.

Unlike the Rat with the Snake, whose Water and Fire produce powerful steam, with the Rat and Horse, Horse's Fire gets promptly put out by Rat's Water. Or else Rat's Water evaporates Horse's Fire into thin air. Theirs is not a productive relationship, so as business partners, it will be difficult for them to achieve success together.

In a marriage, while Rat and Horse are not nearly as destructive as some other Zodiac Enemy couples, nevertheless they will never be well-suited to one another on any level. There will always be that nagging feeling of lack, of the other not living up to the idea of the perfect partner.

In 2020, things get a lot worse, with Rat's temper constantly threatening to go off. Horse meanwhile is petrifying when in a rage, and when Rat and Horse get together, sparks fly but not in a good way. They constantly get at each other's throats and when left together too long, could start being seriously bad for one another.

If Rat and Horse are already in a relationship and want to make things better, they need to use each other's secret friend. The Rat person should carry a **Sheep Amulet**, while the Horse person should carry an **Ox Amulet**.

Alternatively if they are a married couple, if they can form the *Cardinal Cross* with their family members, e.g. if they have two children born under the signs of **Rabbit** and **Rooster**, they transform all negative aspects of their relationship into something auspicious. An easier way is to display the **Cardinal Cross Mirror** featuring all four cardinal animal signs in your home.

157

RAT/SHEEP *Opposites attract*
Rat wrapped around Sheep's little finger

Rat and Sheep are as different as night and day, and in any other year, this pair are unlikely to come together as a couple. But 2020 is different. Sheep's luck far surpasses Rat's, and Rat could well fall for the seductive Sheep who has its eye out for the Rat. The Sheep as a romantic partner is extremely attractive, and even when there appears little common ground, when Sheep sets its sights on somebody, it usually succeeds.

Rat in 2020 will find Sheep very hard to resist! Unlike last year when Sheep was going through a difficult time with the *Five Yellow*, this year, Sheep emerges stronger, more confident and readier to take on the world. And it has Rat eating out of its hand!

The Rat person who gets involved with a Sheep in 2020 could well see the romance turning serious. Marriage between the two is more than possible, and if the relationship does go down that track, it is not all bad. But whether their extremely dissimilar personalities can last the long haul is a different matter. If it works, it will most definitely be a case of opposites attracting.

In Chinese astrological circles, Rat gets attracted to Sheep's seductive wiles, but could find Sheep too manipulative once they are married. Sheep enjoys an attentive Rat partner as long as it can maintain its *femme fatale* ways keeping Rat enthralled. When the initial attraction wears off is when the problems begin.

This coupling works better with Rat as the male, and Sheep as the female. Sheep is likely to be the one pulling the strings from the background, while Rat is happy to let Sheep orchestrate all their common moves. Until Rat wakes up and wants some say as well!

In 2020, Rat and Sheep enjoy an intensely passionate relationship, but it may be better not to get "hooked" despite everything seeming just swell. Over the long term, this is not an ideal pairing. Life could become tedious and both then succumb to looking elsewhere for love. Risk of infidelity could be high for a married Rat and Sheep couple, unless you engage suitable **marriage strengthening cures** and keep each other suitably engaged. But for now, enjoy the ride while it lasts!

Display the Marriage Happiness Ducks in the home to improve marital harmony.

CHAPTER FIVE

RAT/MONKEY *Ally power*
Best of pals on a roll!

Two best friends who always get along like a house on fire whether this is a love, work or family relationship. Rat and Monkey are allies of the Zodiac belonging to the Trinity of Competitors, and no matter what each are going through, they always have each other's backs. They are supportive of one another and think along the same wavelength.

> Between Rat and Monkey, there is little need to communicate through words. They know what the other thinks almost telepathically. When you put a Rat and Monkey together, there is always love, support and a good deal of humour. They are serious about success but do not take themselves too seriously.

In 2020, neither is particularly strong in terms of element luck or other indications, but the 24 Mountains do bring the Monkey a *Big Auspicious* and two *Small Auspicious* stars. For a Monkey going out with a Rat partner, the relationship boosts its confidence, self-esteem and assuredness, allowing Monkey to lift Rat up, gaining success for both. A

Monkey and Rat pairing in 2020 could see both riding very high indeed!

Monkey's Metal produces Rat's Water, so in this pair, it is likely for Monkey to take the lead. Rat gives Monkey whatever back-up it needs to stay strong, creative and action-oriented. And when these two succeed together, they enjoy the fruits of their labour equally. In a Rat and Monkey pairing, there will never be tussling for who gets credit for what. They are mutually supportive of each other and always recognise what the other brings to the table.

This relationship works just as well in business as it does in a marriage. In 2020, Monkey tempers Rat's quarrelsome nature with its wit and humour, while Rat brings Monkey back down to earth when Monkey goes about conconcting one grand scheme after another. Together, their creativity and work ethic allow them to achieve much together.

This pairing works well in the short term, and even better in the long term. If Rat and Monkey get together this year and are wondering if they should take things further and seal the deal, the advice is to go for it! There's little that ever comes between Rat and Monkey. You are superb for each other and enviable well-suited.

CHAPTER FIVE

RAT/ROOSTER *Good for each other*
Much bliss and happiness to be had

Rat and Rooster have a love-hate relationship, but if they get together as a couple, they will be a long-lasting one. There is genuine love between this pair, and even if they may go off at each other and tempers may temporarily flare, they always kiss and make up quickly.

It is not difficult for a Rat and Rooster to find lasting happiness with one another, but usually this requires Rooster to have the upper hand. Rooster will not be happy to play second fiddle to the Rat.

If they can find that kind of rhythm with one another, there is much bliss and happiness to be had in each other's arms.

In 2020, Rooster's luck surpasses that of the Rat, so as always, Rooster should be the one to take the lead. Rooster enjoys some extremely exciting indications from the *24 Mountains Constellation* and if Rat allows Rooster to take charge without too many questions asked, they would save each other a lot of needless fireworks and with much success in the offing.

As work associates or business partners, the Rat and Rooster work better than if they were romantically involved. As workmates, the Rooster is the visionary while the Rat gets things done. This is not a relationship of "equals" in the regular sense of the word. If Rat insists on calling the shots, Rooster's temper is likely to match that of the Rat's this year, and then things could get ugly.

The Rat has the *#3 Quarrelsome Star* which makes it terribly bad-tempered in 2020, but if the two can find a way to calm the tantrums, results come quickly. The good news is that this year, Rooster is feeling calmer and more focused on the work at hand than on picking fights. If Rat can realise this, this relationship can lead to much love and success.

The good thing in this relationship is the ability of Rat and Rooster to operate independently, both being strong enough to stay the course. This is not the most romantic of couples, and with so many challenges facing them this year, it could well lead to a split. This would however be a shame because they are good for each other. To boost chances of things working out, Rat needs the **Anti-Anger Amulet,** while Rooster needs the **Fifteen Hums Protection Wheel** to suppress the troublesome *Yin House* in its sector.

CHAPTER FIVE

RAT/DOG *Love blossoms*

Ho Tu combination brings good fortune

The Rat and Dog, while not the most passionate of couples, enjoy a quiet and contented kind of relationship with one another. While sparks are unlikely to fly between these two, should they get together as a couple, it will not be difficult for them to make things last.

Dog is a Earth animal, happiest when sniffing out new adventures, and with loved ones, loyal to a fault. Rat is far more shrewd and wily, and Dog's holier-than-thou ways could sometimes grate on Rat's nerves. But in 2020, love gets every chance to blossom because their star numbers combine to form the magical *Ho Tu!*

In 2020, Rat and Dog find they have more in common than they may at first have thought. Rat learns to appreciate Dog's dedicated do-gooder ways, while Dog takes a walk on the wild side with the street-smart Rat. Rat's #3 and Dog's #8 bring out a trendsetting trait in them, and together they could well become the hottest couple in town! This year Rat and Dog will enjoy the social scene together, and they become the life of party with no effort at all. Rat's argumentative nature gets totally subdued when together with the happy-go-lucky Dog, while Dog's self-confidence grows in the company of the Rat. Both benefit from the influence of the other, making this a good pairing whether in love, work or play.

The Rat and Dog at work together will see Dog lead the charge this year, as Dog is feeling far stronger and more energised than the Rat. Rat is happy to let Dog take the lead as long as Dog does not expect Rat to lift too many fingers. They are compatible this year as both adopt some of the other's personality traits. Their outlooks jive, if only temporarily, but there is enough time for many wonderful shared experiences and successes.

Whether Rat and Dog can last the long haul however is another matter. The Earth element of the Dog will ultimately harm the Water element of the Rat. They are not naturally compatible as Zodiac signs. If you are looking for some short term fun, or getting involved for a project with a definite term period, by all means go ahead with no holds barred. But if you are thinking of marriage, be sure you are truly compatible before taking the plunge, or you could find yourself locked into what each consider a dull union.

CHAPTER FIVE

RAT/BOAR *Passion ignites*

A happy year for these Water element pals

Rat and Boar share the same intrinsic element of Water, so as friends, they always get along. Even as romantic partners, there is sufficient mutual attraction for them to come together this way. But whether they can survive long as a married couple is another matter. Boar enjoys and expects its creature comforts, and if Rat cannot provide, Boar may find it in other ways.

> Emotionally, they are strongly interdependent, with Rat providing the Yang half of the relationship and Boar contributing the Yin. Their differences merge in perfect balance, and it is easy for each to develop a deep love for the other.

In terms of expectations of family life however, the two differ considerably, and then the question becomes whether it is even possible for them to build together what each considers the perfect home. Boar has extravagant tastes while Rat likes to hoard. Boar prefers tidiness and order, Rat survives in its own "organised" mess. But these are all superficial differences and easy to get around, as long as there is enough money. If affluent, a Rat and Boar couple

are likely to live together, with each having their own private spaces within the home. Both are willing to compromise on shared spaces, as long as they are free to do what they like with their own.

The same goes with their bank accounts. No matter how lovey dovey this pair becomes, best to keep money and income separate or it could become the root of all problems.

This relationship is less complicated if Boar is the main breadwinner of the family, in which case its generous nature makes up for Rat's more careful tendencies. But if Rat is the main provider, Boar's spendthrift ways could really stress out the Rat.

In 2020, it will need to be the Boar (who is going through a much better year) who steers the relationship. Their star numbers blend in a superb fashion, but this translates to compatibility only if Boar plays the dominant role in the union.

The Rat who lets Boar play conductor will find itself in a heaven-sent relationship without a care in the world. But ultimately, Rat's need to be an equal contributor could prove to be the Kryptonite of this particular relationship.

CHAPTER FIVE

CHAPTER

6

RAT'S MONTH BY MONTH LUCK FOR 2020

OVERVIEW FOR THE RAT 2020
Minor obstacles mask hidden gold this year!

Rat encounters a mixed bag this year. While you have *Completion Luck* on your side, you face a number of afflictions that require strong remedies to ensure you can tap all the year has to offer. While you have the support of the *Tai Sui*, you need to contend with the *Facing Three Killings,* which brings obstacles to your pursuits. You also have the troublesome #3 in your sector, which makes you more difficult to get along with.

For greater harmony and for the sake of your health, you must learn to relax and to balance work with play. Don't rile yourself up over the small things, and take time out to pursue personal hobbies and interests outside your work and responsibilities. It also helps to treat yourself to the odd vacation now and then.

The exciting indication for the Rat-born however is that your star number together with the dominant number of the year form the *Sum-of-Ten,* which indicates that despite things being difficult in the short term, hard work and perseverance does pay off. Hang in there when the going gets tough, because there are rewards aplenty to be reaped.

**FENG SHUI ENHANCER
FOR THE RAT**
What the Rat needs in 2020 are the
Sum-Of-Ten Enhancer and the
Tai Sui plaque and **amulet** to keep
the God of the Year on your side.

Keep up your strength - both physical and mental
- by getting enough rest, lying low during months
when your luck and energy are down, and tempering
work stress with other interests and with time spent
just chilling out with friends.

For the Rat, it is never the case that working hard is
working more. Rat always looks at the shortest way
to get the job done. You are hard-working but not the
kind who likes to slog it. Not for you hours and hours
of number crunching; you'd rather write yourself a
program and get a computer to do it for you. When
you spend as much effort devising workable, clever
shortcuts, you preserve your energy and allow yourself
more time to seek out new, profitable directions.

Rat's best months this year are May, July, August and September.

FIRST Month
February 4th - March 5th 2020
Romantic diversions subdue anger

The year begins on a peaceful note but there are already indications of what is to come with an excess of WOOD energy in your sector. The annual 3 is both fuelled and subdued by the visiting Wood #4 star, which causes extremes of emotions in your life. This will affect young Rats more than older Rats. Young Rats falling in love for the first time may find themselves climbing aboard an emotional rollercoaster. Don't get overly invested in new love relationships and always be ruled by the head as much as the heart. If you maintain the upper hand, romance could prove a happy distraction.

Work & Career - *Going well*

Your forte this month will be research and communication. Focus on these and you quickly discover how far you can go. These two skills are dominant now, so if you invest time and effort here, you find some important information you can put to good use, benefitting yourself instantly. A series of happy coincidences allow you to assert your authority with minimal effort. Teamwork brings benefits as things get done in double time, but don't push your collaborators too hard or get too bossy, as not everyone can keep up with you and your newfound energy. Hold your temper if you want to retain the support of those working with you.

Someone you are trying desperately to reach could get in touch out of the blue, or some information you require could make its own way to you. A rare period when things seem to happen even as you think about them!

Business - *Networking Luck*

Successful networking nets you immense benefits and rewards, so work on this! Life hums along smoothly and money-making opportunities come from several sources, so you don't have to worry about which way to turn or what step to take. If you have a lead, stock tip or privileged information, act on it as it will bring plump rewards.

Someone you meet casually can turn out very beneficial, so follow up on leads. Through informal chat, you may discover important information or make valuable contacts. Sometimes a chance encounter just to touch-base can change the course of your life. You don't get where you are by reading books, goggling wikipedia or scouring newspapers. Networking and face-to-face contact play a major part in deciding your year-end net worth.

Relationships - *Effervescent*

A good month for singles looking for love. Matters of the heart take your mind off the heavier responsibilities of life, and have the effect of putting you into a good mood. The male Rat is a real ladies' man, while the female Rat impresses with her notable intellect and superior social skills. You find you don't have to do much chasing, as love comes chasing after you!

For the married Rat, be careful you don't let temptation lead you to do the wrong thing. Predatory third parties could be hovering. The young Rat in a new relationship should watch you don't allow your emotions to run amok. Start your relationship off on good footing and avoid letting it completely take over your life. If you have other obligations, put them first, or if not, then at least equal in your priorities.

Education - *Uncovering new talents*

You are feeling eloquent and getting along with everyone is a walk in the park. Your communication skills are productive and make you a ton of new friends. Your popularity only helps your productivity when it comes to school work, so welcome the company when your pals want to hang out. The young Rat also enjoys the companionship of older friends, especially older siblings. A month of discoveries and uncovering new talents!

SECOND Month
March 6th - April 4th 2020
Quarrelsome indeed!

This month is irksome and filled with quarrels big and small. Infighting with colleagues, friends and superiors foul up the month, but these things are sent to test your patience, so stick your chin out and be resolute. Nothing is as bad as you think. There are however risks of lawsuits and legal entanglements. Try to resolve them out of court and avoid outright confrontation as you may lose since your enemies are stronger.

Do not run foul of the law; some temptations for easy money are out there, but if even if it is a grey area, chances of being caught now are high. Not worth running the risk! Your temper needs controlling; in any disagreement, you think you are right, and even if you are, losing your cool causes more damage than what you get in return.

Work & Career - *Feeling irritable*
You are easily aggravated by other people's lack of consistency or what you deem as incompetence. Yet you'll be banging your head on the proverbial brick wall. Even if they are ineffectual and inept, they will triumph! Flying off the handle and scolding them publicly does no good either. It reflects badly on you while the guilty

party gets off scot-free! This rubs more salt into your wounds! Control your temper and watch out for office politics. So much unnecessary gossip is going on. You know they are time-wasting and even if it does not concern you, careless talk will get you into hot soup. Carry the **Peace Amulet** and place a **Rooster figurine** on your desk, and let the world see you are above the fray.

Business - *Low profile*

Business leader and entrepreneur Rats do better keeping a low profile this month. You are plagued by energies of conflict and if you make yourself too available to others, chances of disagreements and clashes are high. Not a good time to have too much interaction with others. You tend to quarrel with many, from business partners and associates to suppliers and customers, which is no good. Better keep all arguments within control so they don't get blown out of proportion.

Relationships - *Tone down the temper*

Maintain peace and harmony by keeping things simple. Don't fight over small things even if you are right. Chances are high you are wrong, and that will just make matters worse. Show extra consideration to your partner since you are the one in the quarrelsome mood. The energy in you now is the negative sort, so you must not let it use you. You are also more aggressive than usual. Calm down and tone down the rhetoric. They have heard it before and you are playing the same old tune.

Education - *Feisty*

The young Rat is in a feisty mood. You are feeling restless even in the face of plenty to get done at school. Adopting a new hobby to keep you motivated could be the way around the odd energy this month.

Home & Family - *Emotions run high*

At home you hold strong opinions and get annoyed when others don't see eye to eye. Your ability to reason coherently is limited this month and each time you pick a fight, you have to struggle to find the proper words. Yet you get involved in fights at the drop of a hat! If you have young children, know that your bad mood will rub off on them and affect them adversely. Restrain your temper and anger.

FENG SHUI TIP: Control the irritable energies with the **Fire Dragon holding Ksiddigarbha's Fireball.** This feng shui cure suppresses all anger energy and ensures quarrels don't get out of hand. The Dragon is also your astrological ally, so having the image of a Dragon near you always benefits and ensures others stay on your side.

THIRD Month
April 5th - May 5th 2019
Physical ailments weaken you

You're not feeling physically strong and it seems if there's a bug to be caught around town, you're likely to catch it. Boost your immunity by avoiding unnecessary contact with people who are sick or down with infectious ailments. Limit your visits to places like hospitals or where many sick people congregate. A time when you need to boost your *Spirit Essence* as you are also more vulnerable to spiritual attacks. We advise carrying the **Spirit Essence Enhancing Amulet.**

The energies also make you more prone to accidents, so limit the risks you take when driving, travelling or engaging in dangerous sporting activities. This is a month to take health ailments seriously, and to take extra measures to shield yourself from illness. Keep the energy in your home and living spaces yang, switch on more lights and wear bright colours.

Work & Career - *Not so productive*

If you're feeling under the weather, don't try to hide this from those you work with. Plan your work schedule and collaborations better and people will understand. If you need someone to cover for you, they will be happy to do it if you ask nicely. Don't promise more than you can deliver and get rest when you need it. Your mind is not fully on the job and this could cause you to underperform as an effective team member. Make allies at the workplace, especially important during times like these when you may not be at your best. Work at leaving enough time for work, rest and play.

Business - *Growth opportunities*

Business luck is good as you receive outside help from people not from the same industry. Many projects resulting in win-win situations come your way, so negotiations are extremely easy as both parties see the benefits. Joint ventures look promising but avoid too many partners. Too many investors can lead to too many agendas. It is better to start small rather than end up with too many parties on the negotiating table.

Money luck is good so you can invest with peace of mind. Luck seems to favour expansion plans, so go ahead and think big. Boost good business luck with a **Double-Humped Camel**, the best symbol of business success especially for those embarking in growth strategies or moving in new directions.

Relationships -*Lucky in love*

Rats in relationships relish what they have with their partner. If you are married or already settled down, you find your partner hugely supportive of whatever ventures you take on. If you want that endearing support to last, don't neglect to afford your partner the same courtesy!

Single Rats are just as lucky in love, so the advice is to pursue whatever it is you have already started. If you have your sights set on somebody, you can get them if you put your heart into it. Don't try too hard to impress but be genuine about your affection. Since love is in the air for the Rat, this is the most ideal time to propose, get engaged or get married. Those wanting to take things to the next level will not misstep if they get things going now.

Education -*Acquiring new skills*

A good month for the young Rat, who scores high on the popularity stakes. Many are taken by your looks and behaviour. Expand your network and social skills. Extracurricular activities that pique your interest will also help you resume later. Your capacity for learning gets magnified, so many new skills come easily to you. Get involved in as many things as possible; you thrive when you have many things to keep you interested.

FOURTH Month
May 6ᵗʰ - June 5ᵗʰ 2020
Light at the end of the tunnel

Your head is clear and you think in practical terms. You see things and people for what they really are. Few can pull the wool over your eyes this month! Since you are brimming with workable ideas that can instantly be applied to your existing financial structures, try them out. One could well turn out to be a money-spinner. In any case, your ideas can only benefit you.

Those in leadership positions thrive in their role as leader, and those who follow or work for you give you strong and unwavering support. The outlook to anything you start looks fabulous, enriching you not just financially but in other ways as well. Happiness, joy and an extremely motivating month.

Work & Career - *Lots going on*

A busy month at work, but just because you are loaded with projects does not mean you can complete all on time and within budget! You have lots to sink your teeth in and though you are raring to go, bear in mind this translates into more deadlines. If you start feeling stressed out, take time out to relax and try thinking out of the box. Not all traditional, tried and true methods are the best. Exploit new technology. Even if you have spend some time learning it, it will be worth your while. There will be opportunity for travel, and for some of you, crossing the great waters could lead to some major life changes – a re-location, a promotion, a job change. Consider all new opportunities coming your way carefully but do not let yourself get anxious about change. This period, change brings only positive outcomes.

Business - *Change is good*

A good month for starting new things, so new ventures fare well. If you are boss or team leader, this is a good time to begin something new, as anything fresh and innovative stands a good chance of success. Be bold and aim high in your strategies; think of new initiatives and new products to launch. If you maintain a strongly positive outlook, whatever you get involved in seems able to bear fruit quickly. Changes made this month will generally be good, as luck of this kind is on your side.

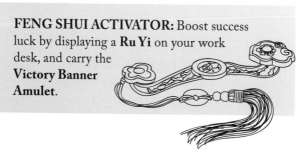

FENG SHUI ACTIVATOR: Boost success luck by displaying a **Ru Yi** on your work desk, and carry the **Victory Banner Amulet**.

Relationships - *Take the initiative*

There is plenty of romance but you need make the effort and take the initiative. You tend to treat your partner lightly and be rather superficial in your outlook. This may work against you, so try to be more loving and sincere. Beware third parties who may enter the picture and risk wrecking your relationship.

CURE: There is danger of infidelity this month, so carry the **Marriage Saver Amulet** and have the **Marriage Happiness Ducks** in the home.

Single Rats could meet someone really special. If someone is interested in you, don't shrug off their advances. Your soulmate may not meet all your usual criteria but if you give them the chance, they could surprise you! Meanwhile, those in stagnant or dead-end relationships should muster up the courage to end things. It is better to not be in a relationship than to be in a bad one. Once you make the break, new love comes knocking more quickly than you think.

Education - *Going well*

Sometimes you put in so much effort only to reap minor rewards, but this month even average time spent on studies seems to push you sky-high! All is going well, so there is little to worry about and plenty of reasons to enjoy.

FIFTH Month
June 6th - July 6th 2020
Misunderstandings detract from month's successes

A good month awaits the Rat, but the quarrelsome star in your chart unfortunately gets worsened by the multiplier effects of the #9. This month will see the Rat even more hot tempered and less tolerant. You become quite the tyrant boss and can be unfair and even unkind in the way you interact with others – especially those lower in status than you. Stop yourself when you catch yourself behaving badly.

Every action has its equal and opposite reaction, and never has Newton's law been more in play.

Work & Career - *Taking stock*

Things are moving quickly and you not only feel super-efficient, you are! You get a lot done, impressing those around you. You have higher than usual levels of energy, which contributes to your new style efficiency and conjures up an almost scary momentum. While it is easy to go with the flow since everything seems to coincide with your plans, it is sometimes necessary to step out of the flow to take stock. Even if the flow appears to take you in the direction you want, no harm done in doing a double check. Or else you will be like wood drift floating aimlessly around, going where the waters take you. Force yourself to stop once in a while to see the wood for the trees.

Business - *Network carefully*

While people you meet now prove important later, you must not go overboard. Do not act on impulse or do anything rash that could embarrass you later. There is no need to let yourself become bosom pals with everyone you meet. In fact, it is better to tread cautiously than be overly approachable and open. Focus on building solid relationships, but remember it is better to cultivate quality than quantity. Be mindful of misunderstandings cropping up. There is success indicated, but for the Rat, your temper and impatience could well become your Achilles' Heel.

Relationships - *Relax*

Let your hair down and hang loose! . The less uptight you are this month, the easier to find true love. Look on the bright side and improve your sense of humour. Life becomes not only easier but more fun this way. Single Rats are poised to find the love of their life, so hang on and keep a lookout for candidates. You are so preoccupied with work your mind tends to dwell on office matters even when dating; so banish all work-related topics from your conversation and concentrate on the task at hand!

Home & Family - *Hosting the extended family*

Expect contact from distant relatives. If they contact you, welcome them with open arms as this is a good time for minor reunions. Invite them over and have a little house party. You will enjoy their company and discover plenty in common. Family ties improve steadily and if you're willing to provide your house and host, your home could become some kind of extended family clubhouse. Perfect for those who are glad for the extra company, for others, this could be too much. Be obliging but learn to draw the line.

Education - *Keeping busy*

Though you may be kept constantly busy at school, you feel inspired enough to try new things and go out on a limb to get to know someone you admire. Great time to take up a hobby. Whatever you start now will enhance your image and make others look up to you. But your mind may wander, so try to manage your time better. Time management is a wonderful tool and once you master it, exhaustion becomes a thing of the past. You feel like taking part in all that is going on, but if you know how juggle your time, a fun time is in store. If not, the bed seems irresistible.

SIXTH Month

July 7th - Aug 7th 2020

Excellent month when everything goes smoothly

A wonderful month when you enjoy not just the *Prosperity Star* but the *Ho Tu* combination that brings victory and leadership luck. Good fortune flows in from multiple directions with plenty of good times in store. The wealth star brings new opportunities to make big money, perhaps even of the windfall kind. Speculation, investments and even playing the lottery could reap handsome rewards!

What you consider sizeable gains will depend on your life situation as everything is relative. But what's clear is that you'll look back and remember this month when most things go your way and plum opportunities fall into your lap. Enjoy, and make the most of this most auspicious time!

ENHANCER: Your luck is very special this month but how special will depend on how well you harness the good fortune luck coming your way. Carry the **Ho Tu Activator Amulet** to get the best out of the month.

Work & Career - *Big break*

A big break may come so keep your eyes peeled for opportunities that may end with a salary increase or commissions. Work on old and new relationships, as someone is in the position to really improve your career. Impressing the right people such as your superiors, directors and VIP customers is important. Your luck crystalizes this month so work on it.

Focusing on good teamwork pays off, and you have the kind of luck that bestows on you very natural leadership luck. Others look to you for guidance, so give it genuinely and wholeheartedly. A promotion is on the cards.

Business - *Closing deals*

This is the perfect time to close contracts, sign deals and finalize all the details. Everything seems to be going your way and people give in to you however outrageous your demands. While they submit to you now, be gracious or they could hold this against you when times are not so rosy. All agreements you make now bear fruit and last for a reasonably long time, so this may well be your heritage to pass on.

Since people can make or break the business, tap on your social skills and undeniable charm. Your sparkling persona when you decide to use it will make you a hit at corporate events and social gatherings. Be pro-active, as a little push is all that is needed to jumpstart your luck, after which it takes on steam on its own and churns out monetary rewards.

Relationships - *Thinking long-term*

You appreciate your partner more as all their good qualities become obvious. While you may have taken them for granted in the past, now you realize you are the lucky one. For the single Rat, while dating is fun, you will be looking for something that can last into the long term. One night affairs do not interest you, so don't bother trying to fill shoes that don't fit. Don't let fear of missing out drive you to do things that don't sit well with you. Peer pressure can be a terrible thing, but you're feeling confident enough to stand your ground and live life by your own standards. A good time for commitment and to take things to another level.

Education - *Goal setting pays off*

There are lots of ways for the young Rat to shine this month. Let one small success lead to another and gradually your achievements will become bigger and bigger. Aim high while making a plan. Set yourself interim goals in pursuit of the ultimate dream. There's a lot going your way, and every goal you set is bound to succeed. And you're focused on schoolwork, you'll find there is still plenty of time for friends.

SEVENTH Month
Aug 8th - Sept 7th 2020
Good fortune luck
brings completion, but stay alert

A promising month but stay careful as you have the violent star #7 paying a visit. This, like the dominant number this year, binds with the #3 in your sector to form the auspicious *sum-of-ten*, so while it brings loss and betrayal, there are hidden benefits. In every obstacle and misfortune you encounter, there is a silver lining. Look for this instead of putting your arms in the air and surrendering.

The energies this month suggest rewards from toil and trouble. Hard work pays off and perseverance even more so.

Good idea to watch whom you trust. Remove temptation where you can. Don't leave the finances to someone else and always stay on top of your game. A time to stay alert.

Work & Career - *Solo-ing it*

You find it more efficient working alone than with others this month. Follow your instincts for there are betrayal energies in the air. Even when someone would rather not cross you or let you down, self-interest could cause them to act out of character. No harm forgiving them, as the energies at this time attract this kind of disappointment. Better not open yourself up to hurt or harm by looking after your own responsibilities yourself. Don't depend on anyone to pass a message for you unless you want the Chinese Whisper treatment applied. It may even be better to rely on those who don't know you so well, so they do not know your weaknesses.

Business - *Stay out of anything new*

You're at risk of getting cheated or conned. You may think this is the last thing you will allow to happen but even hardened business tycoons get cheated so this is just another sad fact of life. Best is not to trust others easily even if you are usually good at judging character. Some investments or purchases made some time ago may turn sour and you end up with a loss. If the loss is minimal or manageable, look on the bright side, grit your teeth and ride it out.

Avoid new joint ventures and stay out of anything new. Do not interfere in other people's affairs or problems; you are in no position to help. If you can maintain the status quo, thank your lucky stars. Conserve money and energy and focus on finishing what you started rather than starting up anything new.

Relationships - *Tread carefully*

Not a good month for those looking for love. Bide your time. If you take a chance and hook up with someone now, probability of it lasting is low. You could find excitement in the form of the occasional dinner date, but if you're hoping it will turn into something more, next month holds more promise. Forcing things to happen too quickly will only lead to disappointment. As with other areas in your life, tread carefully in matters of the heart. For the married Rat, give your partner some space. Smothering your better half with too much affection could drive a wedge between you.

Education - *Start assignments early*

The young Rat has it better than other Rats. You have completion luck on your side, so make the most of it and get your projects wrapped and handed in. Start your assignments as soon as they are set to avoid undue stress the night before a deadline.

FENG SHUI CURE: Carry the **Anti-Robbery Amulet** this month to stay safe from petty thieves and to minimize loss of money for whatever reason.

EIGHTH Month
Sept 8th - Oct 7th 2020
Unexpected support brings good news

A lucky month ahead with no shortage of people stepping forward to help you just when it is needed. This month the luck of *gui ren* falls into your lap. Those in a position to help you choose to do so. Accept any support you get with good grace, stay humble and you can go far. Life is a journey and one never stops learning. For the Rat, there are many useful lessons this month. All of the positive kind.

The Rat enjoys healthy doses of heaven luck with new opportunities and helpful people materializing quite unexpectedly. Things move quickly, so when opportunities open up, don't spend too long mulling things over. Act fast!

Work & Career - *Bold moves*

This period allows you to be courageous and to take some risks. After a tentative last month, you can make your moves with confident decisiveness. You have promotion luck so you can start cosying up to the powers that be. You are in your boss' good books so any discussion about an upgrade is favourably received. Colleagues support you and when necessary, will put in a good word on your behalf. Projects get completed on time and success comes easily. No need to question everyone's motifs; most of the world is on your side. And those that are not will not get very far.

Business - *A time for growth initiatives*

Reaching out for your dreams is a practical exercise since the success rate is high. You can be brave in your endeavours but listen to what others have to say. Even in casual conversation, you stand to glean plenty of useful information that can make the difference between a good and great outcome. People look up to you and your leadership luck is maintained so you can manage with confidence without worrying about anyone's motives.

Financially you are in a strong position and can carry out expansion plans confidently. If you can find ways to expand your business, this is a good time to set things in motion. Luck is on your side, but get going before the month is up. Your luck now is far superior to next month. Things are looking good, but time is of the essence.

Relationships - *Matchmaker matchmaker!*

Those not yet in a steady relationship who are looking

for that special someone should not be averse to getting some help from "matchmakers". Whether trying out a dating app, or engaging the services of an aunt, friend or colleague, who knows what can happen when universal forces are on your side? All you need to do is to make sure you're not dating an iffy character; once you have that assurance, see whether you have anything in common. Energies work in mysterious ways, and when the *Heaven Star* has a strong influence on your chart, things develop in a cosmic almost magical way.

Education - *Showcasing talents*
A great time to forge new friendships, as friends you make now will be with you for years to come and may even play a pivotal role in your life in the near future. For the young Rat, guidance from an older person will be incredibly useful. Those in positions of responsibility are given a real chance to shine, while those perfecting a skill get the chance to showcase their talents. Seize the opportunities that come to you. You can make meaningful leaps and bounds now, so work hard and go forth with purpose. Those with clearly-defined goals will find them surprisingly easy to achieve this month.

NINTH Month

Oct 8th - Nov 6th 2020
Energy turns foul.
Need to be very careful.

The *Five Yellow* makes its way into your chart, bringing all kinds of obstacles and misfortune. Avoid taking risks. Arguments get heated and blown out of proportion unless you make a conscious effort to nip them in the bud. Don't get yourself into petty disagreements and don't try to fight someone else's battles for them. You may encounter a few bad situations, so you take extra caution. This month you should keep a low profile and avoid doing anything of major consequence. Maintaining the status quo is the way to go.

REMEDY: Carry the **Five Element Pagoda Amulet** to dispel the negative energies of the *wu wang* star. Wear the colour white to weaken the malevolent earth element energies of the *wu wang*.

Work & Career - *Beware offices politics*

This is a vulnerable time for the working Rat when you could suffer from politicking or bad-mouthing. Although certain individuals may be outwardly supportive, there is hidden treachery and deceit. You are afflicted by the misfortune star, and combined with the annual argument star, this could lead to your being vulnerable to being undermined or side-lined. You need to be astute to stay on top of your game. Things ease up next month, but for now, watch your back and stay on the ball at all times.

> **TIP:** Display the **Power Ru Yi** and wear **King Gesar's Victory Ring** to maintain your influence and status at the workplace, and to protect yourself from harmful politicking.

Business - *Stay conservative*

Proceed cautiously even if the deal seems fail-proof. There are loopholes galore! Any money making offers can turn out to be underhanded. If you fall foul of the law, it can get nasty as you are open to arrows of misfortune. Put big plans on hold that involve financing from the banks or statutory bodies. They go strictly by the book if you have problems with repayments. Your investment radar is sadly out of focus so don't play the stock market. Big investments can lead to big losses, so this is not the time for risk-taking of any kind.

Relationships - *Keep your feet on the ground*
Don't be overly keen when it comes with forming
relationships, especially of the romantic kind. You
may meet with problems in the form of an abundance
of romantic feeling, but whatever romance you start
up this month could lack staying power.

For those looking for the perfect partner, keep your
feet on the ground. Staying single could be better
than hooking up with the wrong person. Take the
advice of family and close friends. Even if something
is not right for you, your judgement tends to be
clouded and flawed this month. While following your
heart is something you must ultimately do, let your
head have some say as well.

Education - *Hard work needed*
Not the best of times and the young Rat
feels the effects of the *wu wang* as much
as the older ones. You may not be feeling
on top of your game, but hard work and
determination will help you stay afloat.
Your efforts may seem to go unnoticed,
but it could be your disposition that's
getting in your way. Stay positive and you
should get through the month just fine.
Carry the **Education Amulet** to help you
in your studies.

TENTH Month
Nov 7th - Dec 6th 2020
Matters of the heart dominate

Those looking for love find it easily. Even those not particularly looking could see love come knocking on your door, then the ball's in your court to reciprocate or not. Relationships do not always start how you expect, so don't dismiss someone of interest just because they do not check all the boxes. True love blossoms in mysterious ways. A good time to put more effort into any relationship.

Work & Career - *Relationships matter*
It won't be just relationships of a romantic nature that feature prominently now - those you have with your colleagues, bosses and associates all become more important than ever. Your work productivity becomes more dependent on relationships with those you work with; the better you click, the better your combined output.

At work, firm friendships begin to take root. They could be with co-workers you barely knew before, or even a former nemesis who strangely becomes a friend. You're much more amenable to letting others into you inner circle, and when you do, you find this not just makes you more efficient, it also makes working life more enjoyable.

The only danger is the romantic star, which brings opportunity of an office romance to blossom. Play it smart and don't let your guard down no matter how much your head is turned. Others can be extremely flattering, but maintain your professionalism or there could be unwelcome consequences.

Business - *Getting creative*

This month will be about finding new directions to explore. The bread and butter of the business will be running itself and now you have time to take a breather to see what other areas you may want to go into. This is the most fun part of the job! The trick is to allow others to take over from you in areas that already run like clockwork so you can turn your attentions to developing new ideas.

WOOD element energy dominates the month, indicating growth potential for any business with a Rat person at the helm. Wood signifies growth, which is why in feng shui we are always so fond of healthy, vibrant plants in the spaces we live in. We design a number of wealth trees each year to symbolise prosperity and growth energy. Display these **wealth trees** in the SE of your office to tap the growth energies of the month.

Relationships - *Getting serious*

For the single Rat, this could be a month for getting serious and taking things to the next level. You may have been playing the field, but now you're tired of the chase and looking forward to settling down. If your potential steady partner has not made the moves, you should do it. The Rat has good energy levels, so take the lead if something feels right for you.

The married Rat however should beware excessive *Peach Blossom* energy. The overdose of romantic energies may cause a 7-year itch or similar. So watch your spouse. Infidelities sometimes happen unintentionally, and then the damage is done and you have to deal with it, or just as bad if you end up having to keep a dirty secret. Knowing this, approach this month with a lot of care, and more attention on your spouse. Don't let the chemistry between you stagnate or cause either of you to look elsewhere for love.

Education - *Everything falling into place*

The #4 does not just bless those looking for love, it is also the star that bestows intellect, brainpower and success in academic studies. The young Rat should do everything to make the most of this good fortune this month!

ELEVENTH Month
Dec 7*th* 2020 - Jan 5*th* 2021
Keep tight leash on your short fuse

You're terribly quarrelsome, even if you're by nature quite patient. The #3 star has been wreaking all kinds of havoc through the year but this month its strength gets doubled. Others could pick fights with you for no apparent reason at all. There may be lawsuits to deal with or problems with the authorities.

The only thing you can do to calm the confrontational energies is to lie low. Don't take the bait when irked. Spend the month as quietly as possible. As for disagreements, this is not the time to attempt any reconciliation; you're more likely to end up souring the relationship further.

Work & Career - *Minimise interaction*
You work better alone than too closely with others now. With less interaction, you reduce the possibility of quarrels and misunderstandings. Too much discussion and too many meetings can be counter-productive. Refrain from acting on impulse; angry words uttered in the heat of the moment cannot be taken back and could lead to dismal consequences.

A month when you may be better off clearing some leave and going on holiday.

Business - *Misunderstandings*
The most pressing problems come from misunderstandings, so when you find yourself in this kind of position, try making your stand clear. Let everyone know your stance from the beginning so no miscommunications occur. The air of hostility seems pervasive and will be hard to dispel, so try living with it. Your charm levels are also at a low ebb, and try as you might, you appear less than attractive compared to your usual self. Don't worry; this is temporary. Avoid trying to close big deals. Your ideas seem to lack appeal. If there are important pitches, let others do the job.

Relationships - *Argumentative*
Not a peaceful month when it comes to love and personal relationships. The better you know someone, the worse it becomes. Don't let things get out of hand. Nip quarrels in the bud and stop yourself arguing over nothing. If you make an effort to find middle ground in any disagreement, things go a lot better. Not a good month for getting engaged or married.

Home & Family Life - *Have more patience*

Be patient with family, especially older members like parents and young ones like kids. You fly off the handle at the slightest provocation and blame them for pressing the panic button. But it is you, not them, so try to be less irritable. As long as you are aware of your current disposition, you are more able to cope. You can improve your mood quite easily if you put in a little effort.

Education - *Tiresome*

A tiresome month for the young Rat, but if you lie low, you can sail through with minimal effort. Better to spend time working alone than trying to get work done with pals - you'll end up arguing more than getting any real work done. Falling out with friends may get you down, but don't let temporary blips get you down. The tides will turn next month and you'll wonder why you were fighting in the first place.

Friendships - *Mind your own business*

Don't try to get involved in what everyone else is doing. You're stubborn this month, and friends and family are unlikely to want your advice. There will be far more harmony in all your relationships if you let everyone get on with their own business without trying to get butt in.

TWELFTH Month
Jan 6th - Feb 3rd 2021
Feeling under the weather

Take better care of yourself. The illness star makes
you more vulnerable to falling sick and feeling
generally quite poorly. The #2 also brings greater
risk of accidents and injuries, so those involved in
rough sports should be more careful. When you feel
your energy levels dipping, make time to recharge.
Ignoring what your body is telling you could just get
you more sick and force you into bed, which would be
far more frustrating. Your tendency to be quarrelsome
subsides, but there may still be traces, so continue to
make every effort to stay calm and agreeable.

Work & Career - *Show some fight*

All may not be well on the work front. Others vying
for your position may use this time when you're not
operating at your best to play politics. Stay alert to
pals who may be wolves in Sheep's clothing. While
you want to stay above the fray, don't try to be too
honourable or always play the good guy, especially if
you come under attack. No one respects a loser who
just steps aside. Show some fight! You have plenty of
that in your reserves, just make sure it is used against
the right person.

Business - *Avoid risk-taking*

Stay low profile as there are risks to your reputation. Appearing too successful will attract jealous rivals who may try sabotage your efforts or taint your good name. Better not to trust others too easily. Even friends can let you down, sometimes not intentionally, so beware with this as your luck is not great.

Avoid risky investments. Don't speculate on the stockmarket no matter how well you think you know your game. Look at preserving your money rather than how you can spend it.

Relationships - *Many admirers*

Luck in love is better than elsewhere so this is a major consolation in an otherwise dreary period. Rats looking for love find it easily. You have many admirers and all the attention puts you back into a good mood despite your lower energy levels. In fact, turning more attention to your relationships helps to revive you and breathe life into an otherwise lowly month. Accept invitations to parties and enjoy yourself. After all the wear and tear at the office, this is a welcome respite.

Health - *Stay away from yin places*

Health luck is poorly and you find yourself more susceptible to falling ill. Wear **health amulets** to ward off illness vibes. Avoid mixing too much with friends who are sick; you're likely to catch whatever they have, and have it worse as your immunity is quite low. This is a time when you should give priority to your health, so if something is not feeling right, better to go see a doctor and get yourself checked out.

Put attention to developing a healthier regime including a well-balanced diet, exercise and enough sleep. Stay away from hospitals and places that emit too much yin energy.

Education - *Pomodoro your work*

The illness star makes it harder to concentrate, and even the young Rat starts to feel the effects of fatigue more quickly. If schoolwork becomes hard to manage, try the Pomodoro technique - split your work into small chunks of 25 minutes then take a 5 minute break. You'll find it easier to keep alert and focused.

*for more on all the recommended
feng shui cures, remedies & enhancers for*

2020

please log on to

www.fsmegamall.com/2020

for more on feng shui, visit

www.wofs.com

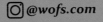 **@wofs.com**